M000281043

VOICE
The Secret Power of Great Writing

VOICE

The Secret Power of Great Writing

James Scott Bell

Compendium Press

Copyright © 2015 James Scott Bell
All rights reserved.

Compendium Press
P.O. Box 705
Woodland Hills, CA 91365

ISBN 10: 0-910355-28-2
ISBN 13: 978-0-910355-28-5

Table of Contents

What is Voice Anyway?

In 1964 the United States Supreme Court decided a case called *Jacobellis v. Ohio*. It was a First Amendment dispute. The state of Ohio had banned the showing of a French movie. French movies in those days were almost guaranteed to disturb the sensibilities of farmers and small town merchants, and the state was empowered to ban what it considered "obscene."

This was the question the Court faced: Was this French film, with its unapologetic visual homage to the unclothed feminine form, so explicit as to render it obscene? If it was not, then Ohio would be prohibited by the First Amendment from banning it.

The Court ultimately held that Ohio had overstepped its bounds, but when it came to the definition of obscenity, the justices found themselves all over the place. It was the concurring opinion of Justice Potter Stewart that rendered a now famous quote. He said he could not define obscenity, but "I know it when I see it."

Which is exactly how most publishing professionals feel about *voice* in fiction. It defies definition, but we all know it when we see it.

In this book, I want to help you "see" voice. I want you to see it in the writing of others, but more importantly I want to help you find it and let it run free in your own writing.

Because voice is the "secret power" of great writing.

It can take a pretty good novel and make it unforgettable.

It can take a pretty good author and up their game like almost nothing else.

And you need that in your fiction these days, because there is plenty of good writing out there. The competency level of writers is higher than ever. Over the last couple of decades we've seen an explosion of books, articles, blogs, critique groups, conferences, and other resources covering the art of fiction. The diligent students of the craft are guaranteed to improve.

But if you want to stand out, grow an audience, and have readers seeking your new work, then make it your aim to transcend the competent.

Marian Lizzi, who at the time of this writing is editor-in-chief of Perigee Books (an imprint of Penguin Group USA) once wrote about reasons a submitted book gets turned down by a publishing company. Among them was the following:

> **Not remarkable/surprising/unputdownable enough.** This one is the most difficult to articulate – and yet in many ways it's the most important hurdle to clear. Does the proposal get people excited? Will sales reps and buyers be eager to read it – and then eager to talk it up themselves?
>
> As my first boss used to warn us green editorial assistants two decades ago, the type of submission that's the toughest to spot – and the most essential to avoid -- is the one that is "skillful, competent, literate, and ultimately forgettable."

That's the reason voice is crucial. It takes you from skillful, competent, literate, and forgettable to the kind of book we all love to find—unputdownable.

Still, industry pros have difficulty figuring out what voice is, even as they say they want more of it. Every time there's a panel of agents or editors at a conference, when they are asked what they're looking for in a manuscript, someone always says, "A fresh voice."

But no one can agree what that is.

Over the years I've heard some attempts at explanation, and I've jotted them down:

- A combination of character, setting, page turning.
- A distinctive style, like a Sergio Leone film.

- It's who you are.
- Personality on the page.
- It's something written from your deepest truth.
- Your expression as an artist.

You'll often hear these same people say they turned down a book because the voice was "weak."

So heck, how do you find your voice when the very definition is so vague? Is it something that can be developed? Or is it something you're just born with?

What if you write in different genres? Is your voice in a noir thriller going to be the same as your voice in a romance?

This book is an attempt to answer those questions, but even more to give you practical tools and techniques for coaxing voice out of your writer's mind and spirit.

In one of my favorite movies of all time, *The Treasure of the Sierra Madre*, Humphrey Bogart plays a down and out American in Mexico. He partners up with another transient to go find gold in the mountains. An old prospector (played by Walter Huston in an Oscar-winning role) comes along to provide the experience.

At one point they get to a stream and the prospector shows the other two men how to pan for gold. Some sand and some water, and then a little bit of swishing. He warns them not to be too strong with it. "Gold ain't like stones in a river bank," he says. "It don't call out to be picked up. You got to know how to recognize it. And the finding ain't all. Not by a long shot. You got to know how to tickle it so it comes out laughing."

Let's start tickling.

The CAP Method
for Dynamic Voice

In this chapter I'm going to reveal where true voice in fiction comes from. It's a place almost everyone misses. That's because in virtually all discussions about this mysterious thing called *voice* it is assumed that it is the *author's* voice we're talking about.

> *She has such a memorable voice.*
> *He has a voice you won't soon forget!*

And then the new writer strikes out to see if he has some kind of *voice* as he writes his story. And, not finding it, gets frustrated.

The frustration comes because voice does not come from the author.

Yes, I said that.

This thing called voice does not (except on rare occasions that I discuss in the next chapter) proceed from the author alone.

Every author needs help.

From whom?

From the character.

The real secret, the main thing I want you to take away from this book, is this:

CHARACTER background and language filtered through the AUTHOR'S heart, and rendered with craft on the PAGE = VOICE

This is the crucial dynamic, the big reveal, and it will keep you from being frustrated in the quest to "find your voice."

I call this the CAP Method.

C is for Character.

A is for Author.

P is for Page.

The first two aspects, character and author, are *symbiotic*. That is, they exist in union and grow together. After that stage of growth comes the final destination on the page, rendered through the craft of the writer. The process looks like this:

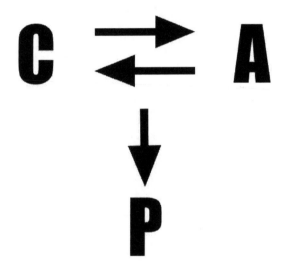

Let's take a look at each step.

Character

When we read a novel that has a memorable voice, we are not reading an author's memoir. Even if the novel is autobiographical, it is a novel because it is about characters. Usually, one character dominates—the Protagonist (or my preferred term, Lead).

To create a memorable voice you must first create a memorable character.

Of course, you may have different chapters or scenes where another character takes the Point of View. In that case, follow the CAP Method for each.

There are many approaches to creating characters, and innumerable craft books and blogs on the topic. Some writers like to write long character biographies, or fill out a dossier of questions covering all aspects of a character's background.

Other writers like to grab a quick idea and let the character grow as they write.

For our purposes, let me offer you a simple way to get the voice of the character into your own head. This, to me, is by far the most important part of the character creation process.

What you need are the answers to five key questions, then a visual, and finally a voice journal.

Five key questions

Before I begin fleshing out a main character, I need to answer these five questions:

1. What is my character's dominant impression?

The great writing teacher Dwight V. Swain explained dominant impression as an adjective of manner connected to a noun of vocation.

_____	+	_____
adjective of manner		noun of vocation

You start with the noun. What is your character's main role in life?

Doctor?

Lawyer?

Mother?
Thief?

Now attach an adjective of manner to the character. How does that character come across to people that know him?
Sloppy?
Slick?
Driven?
Drunk?

Let's say you wanted to write a story about a couple of cops who are paired up, and don't want to be.

One of them is a *straight-laced detective* on the verge of retirement.

You decide to make the other detective reckless and even a little bit crazy. In fact, his antics might get the straight-laced cop killed.

So what kind of cop would that be?

How about a *suicidal cop?*

Perfect! You've just laid the foundation for *Lethal Weapon*.

Unfortunately, it's already been written and filmed.

But you have a million other choices.

The dominant impression is the first question to answer.

2. What is my character's physical appearance?

What does the character look like? Get down all the obvious features: hair, eyes, height, weight, body type, marks, tattoos, scars, and distinguishing features.

3. What is my character's basic background?

Flesh out the following:

Where did my character grew up?
What kind of family life?
What economic conditions?
What level of education?

What music, movies, and other pop culture items were important to her as a young girl? A teenager?

4. What life-altering event happened to my character at age sixteen?

I've found this to be a powerful question in formulating character. Age sixteen is such an emotional one for most of us. Create an event that happened to your character that has emotional reach into her present.

If your character is a minor, you can just move the question back to age seven. Or whatever seems to fit.

5. What does my character yearn for?

I want to know what my character dreams of, desires to do or possess. What is it my character lacks that can only be filled by this yearning?

There are, of course, many other questions you might prefer to address. I like to give my characters a little breathing room to develop along the way, and getting too detailed at this point limits me.

A visual

Once I have these basic questions answered, I know a heck of a lot about my character. I have the physical description in my head, but now I want more.

I want to see the character in front of me.

So I go on an image search.

I type key terms into the Google Images search box, and keep looking until a face jumps out at me, hits me with a feeling that *this is my character.*

I save that image so I can look at it before I start my daily writing.

Note: I use Scrivener for my drafts, and create a cast of characters with head shots so I can see them all together on a corkboard. I find this invaluable for getting ready to write a scene.

A Voice Journal

Finally, you want to *hear* the character in his own, distinct voice.

I use a Voice Journal for this. The VJ is a free-form document, written entirely in the character's voice. You can prompt the character with questions, or just let them run on about whatever topic pops into "their" heads.

Of course it's you doing everything, but you want to unleash your wild right brain and let things be said that you don't try to control.

The point of the VJ is to hear your character talking to you in a different voice than your own.

Also, in a way that is not stereotypical.

Let me give you a couple of examples.

Suppose my character is an elderly woman whose neighborhood is rapidly changing. The VJ might start out like this:

> Don't get me started, do NOT get me started! Kids have no respect, they are being raised by mothers who take drugs all the time. The only drug I ever took was aspirin and that was enough for me. I don't want to hear any excuses for any of this nonsense. Do you know what I used to do, young man? I used to count money for a concession stand on the Santa Monica Pier, and believe you me I saw things. I saw all sorts of things, and it was all a very friendly place until the hippies came along, all dirty and smelly, and they smoked dope all the livelong day. It was their choice to do it, and if you want my opinion they should have all been dragged out to sea and given a bath then shipped off to Mexico. That's right, that's what I said, and now we have the kids in this neighborhood running across my lawn and tearing up the flowers and not caring, you know why? Because they have drugs in their blood, passed down to them by their hippie grandparents!

Or an LAPD cop who is beginning to regret his career choice:

> So yeah, I been a cop fourteen years, and they get to you after awhile, the brass, they don't back you up, you get a form in your file. Then you come home and bam, you can't let it go. My wife couldn't deal with it, so she left, we're still friends and all, but I got a little girl I only see every other weekend. That's crap. But I figure she's better off with her mother.
>
> I go sometimes to the skating rink and I don't even skate. Never could. My ankles always turned in, my dad would laugh at me for that. So I laugh at other people all the time. It takes the edge off. They don't know I'm laughing, so what harm does it do? Guy fell down the steps at City Hall the other day. Homeless guy, one of those, you know? Down he goes, right in front of a bunch of people. Some woman goes over to help him.
>
> Me, I laughed.

My VJs can go on for pages. I'll come back to them and add to them from time to time. But I know I've hit pay dirt when the voice I'm hearing is surprising to me.

At this point you've accomplished a lot, and in a very short time. A great character voice is starting to emerge. Now add the next powerful element to the mix.

I'm talking about *you.*

Author

A great voice is symbiotic. You, the author, must identify with the character so closely that you feel what the character feels, think what the character thinks.

This is what great actors do. In my own acting days I was privileged to study with two of the best teachers in America, Uta Hagen and her disciple Tracy Roberts. In her book, *Respect for Acting,* Hagen expounds on the principle of *substitution.* In brief, you research the character you're going to play then find ways to put your own emotional and sense memories into the part.

Every emotion any character feels in a play you have also felt to one degree or another. The essence of the actor's art is to go back into their own life and find similar feelings, then magnify them and appropriate them for the role.

To illustrate, Hagen used the example of an actress preparing to play Blanche DuBois in *A Streetcar Named Desire.*

> I have to hunt for an understanding of—and an identification with—the character's main needs: a need for perfection (and always *when* and *how* have I needed these things); a romantic need for beauty; a desire for gentleness, tenderness, delicacy, elegance, decorum; a need to be loved and protected; a strong sensual need; a need for delusion when things go wrong, etc.

Hagen then notes that there is a vast difference between herself and Blanche. Hagen considered herself an "earthy, frank, gutsy child of nature." Blanche, of course is the exact opposite. So what to do?

Hagen reached back to remember a night when she prepared for an evening at the opera. She bathed in scented water, soothing her skin, brushed her hair until it was shining. She artfully applied makeup "until the little creases are hidden and my eyes look larger and I feel younger."

She recalled weeping over a poem by Rilke, how her flesh "tingled" at a Schubert chamber piece, the "tender" feelings a soft twilight brought out in her.

All these she applied to Blanche, filtered through her own life experience.

That's how the two became one.

Symbiosis.

So try this. Define your character with five key emotions, and two life-altering events.

Key emotions might be: playful, fearful, angry, lost, suspicious, loving. Use both positive and negative emotions. You want your character to be complex.

A life-altering event is something you dream up for your character. I like to use the age sixteen incident (described above). Then I create another key moment, like the first time the character fell in love, or her first job.

Now, go over each word and find in your own past a moment when you felt the same thing. Relive that past moment by remembering the sights, sounds, touches, and smells. Dwell on them until you feel the emotions afresh.

[Note: take your time with this exercise. You will be amazed at how the emotions come back to you. We did this once in a Tracy Roberts class, where she asked us to remember a time when we were laughing. I went back to a college incident involving my roommate, copious amounts of beer, riding bicycles in our apartment and trying to throw darts at our dart board—and missing every time. I didn't force any laughter, just remembered the smells, sounds, touch, and sights. The laughter snuck up on me, and was so real and extended Tracy stopped the others and had her video guy just film me. I wonder whatever happened to that tape?]

Now, write a paragraph on your thoughts about each of those memories.

Next, identify with each of the two life-altering events. Think back to a time when you felt the same way the character must have. Re-create those emotions using the same memory exercise as above.

Write a page about how you felt at each of those times.

At the end of this process you will practically be the character (in an actor's sense), and the voice that emerges will be strong, true, complex, unique.

That's the power of symbiosis.

Page

The final step in all this is the writing. You want to get that voice, vibrating with your own feelings, on the page.

Which means *feeling something as you write.*

But how?

I am going to offer you one more acting exercise, one of

the best I ever came across. This exercise is credited to a famous theatre director named Michael Chekhov. It comes from his book, *To the Actor.*

It's called the *psychological gesture.* The foundation for this exercise comes from the fact that our physiology informs our psychology. For example, if you put a big smile on your face you're going to feel just a little bit happier than you did the moment before. It might be just a touch more, but it will be enough to prove the point.

Conversely, if you shrink your body and hang your head and take all expression off your face, you're going to feel a little bit darker than you did the moment before.

Try it. Plaster your mug with a big smile, like you're an insurance salesman meeting a prime prospect. Now, with that smile fixed, say, "Murder, death, and destruction are everywhere. Life is a hell hole. I hate life."

You felt pretty silly saying that, didn't you? Your physiology was affecting your psychology.

Try it the other way. Hang your head, remove all expression from your face, and say, "I'm the happiest person on earth!"

Chekhov's great insight was that an actor could take on a physical position that would immediately make him feel like the character. The physicality of it was like an abstract painting. In other words, the actor puts his whole body into a form that creates the inner life of the character.

In the book, Chekhov gives several examples. Here's one:

> [I]magine a character entirely attached to an earthly kind of life. Its powerful and egotistical will is constantly drawn downward. All its passionate wishes and lusts are stamped with low and base qualities. It has no sympathy for anyone or anything. Mistrust, suspicion and blame fill its whole limited and introverted inner life. The character denies a straight and honest way of living, always choosing roundabout and crooked paths. It is a self-centered and at times an aggressive type of person.

The actor would then find a psychological gesture that creates this type of person inside himself. The illustration given in the book looks like this:

It's a simple, quick, but powerful exercise.

Using all the information you have gathered so far, write out a summary paragraph like the one above.

Then use your body to find a position that makes you *feel* it. Play around with different poses until one of them strikes you. One will, and soon.

Remember to keep it abstract.

Now, whenever you get ready to write a scene, take a moment to strike the pose.

Feel it.

Then write.

What if you're in a public place? You can close your eyes and *imagine* you are taking the pose. It still works.

That's the CAP Method. It's not complicated, it's not time consuming. You can do all of this in a couple of hours. But the payoff is permanent: the voice you create will be the foundation for an unputdownable novel.

When the Voice is the Author

There are novels, of course, where the voice of the author does indeed take center stage.

For example, in the comic novels that make up *The Hitchhiker's Guide to the Galaxy* series, no one doubts we are hearing the voice of Douglas Adams. His intent is to make us laugh and think and be entertained all at the same time. He wants us to see the crazy universe he has created via his own, amused outlook.

> The history of the Galaxy has got a little muddled, for a number of reasons: partly because those who are trying to keep track of it have got a little muddled, but also because some very muddling things have been happening anyway.
> One of the problems has to do with the speed of light and the difficulties involved in trying to exceed it. You can't. Nothing travels faster than the speed of light with the possible exception of bad news, which obeys its own special laws. The Hingefreel people of Arkintoofle Minor did try to build spaceships that were powered by bad news but they didn't work particularly well and were so extremely unwelcome whenever they arrived anywhere that there wasn't really any point in being there. (*Mostly Harmless* by Douglas Adams)

When an author's narrative voice is clear and even intrusive, we call it the Omniscient Point of View.

This POV was much more prevalent in the 19th and early

20th centuries. Take this famous opening of *A Tale of Two Cities* by Charles Dickens, published in 1859:

> It was the best of times, it was the worst of times, it was the age of wisdom, it was the age of foolishness, it was the epoch of belief, it was the epoch of incredulity, it was the season of Light, it was the season of Darkness, it was the spring of hope, it was the winter of despair, we had everything before us, we had nothing before us, we were all going direct to Heaven, we were all going direct the other way—in short, the period was so far like the present period, that some of its noisiest authorities insisted on its being received, for good or for evil, in the superlative degree of comparison only.
>
> There was a king with a large jaw and a queen with a plain face, on the throne of England; there were a king with a large jaw and a queen with a fair face, on the throne of France. In both countries it was clearer than crystal to the lords of the State preserves of loaves and fishes, that things in general were settled for ever.

This is Dickens with an opening commentary as he is about to unfold a sweeping historical drama. His opinions are apparent (e.g., the appearance of the queen of England) as well as his subtle humor ("...the State preserves of loaves and fishes...")

When Dickens begins the narrative, he pulls back from overt commentary. But the Omniscient style allows him to float wherever he wants in the scene, observe things from "above" as it were.

> The passenger booked by this history, was on the coach-step, getting in; the two other passengers were close behind him, and about to follow. He remained on the step, half in the coach and half out of; they remained in the road below him. They all looked from the coachman to the guard, and from the guard to the coachman, and listened. The coachman looked back and the guard looked back, and

even the emphatic leader pricked up his ears and looked back, without contradicting.

The stillness consequent on the cessation of the rumbling and labouring of the coach, added to the stillness of the night, made it very quiet indeed. The panting of the horses communicated a tremulous motion to the coach, as if it were in a state of agitation. The hearts of the passengers beat loud enough perhaps to be heard; but at any rate, the quiet pause was audibly expressive of people out of breath, and holding the breath, and having the pulses quickened by expectation.

You can tell this is Omniscient because the author describes things in a way that the characters themselves cannot see. For example, the report that *all* their hearts are beating.

A strength of the Omniscient POV is that the author can describe a character in such a way as to set him immediately in our minds. One of the best at this was Sinclair Lewis, who describes the titular character of his novel *Babbitt* this way:

His name was George F. Babbitt. He was forty-six years old now, in April, 1920, and he made nothing in particular, neither butter nor shoes nor poetry, but he was nimble in the calling of selling houses for more than people could afford to pay.

His large head was pink, his brown hair thin and dry. His face was babyish in slumber, despite his wrinkles and the red spectacle-dents on the slopes of his nose. He was not fat but he was exceedingly well fed; his cheeks were pads, and the unroughened hand which lay helpless upon the khaki-colored blanket was slightly puffy. He seemed prosperous, extremely married and unromantic; and altogether unromantic appeared this sleeping-porch, which looked on one sizable elm, two respectable grass-plots, a cement driveway, and a corrugated iron garage. Yet Babbitt was again dreaming of the fairy child, a dream more romantic than scarlet pagodas by a silver sea.

For years the fairy child had come to him. Where

25

others saw but Georgie Babbitt, she discerned gallant youth. She waited for him, in the darkness beyond mysterious groves. When at last he could slip away from the crowded house he darted to her. His wife, his clamoring friends, sought to follow, but he escaped, the girl fleet beside him, and they crouched together on a shadowy hillside. She was so slim, so white, so eager! She cried that he was gay and valiant, that she would wait for him, that they would sail—

Rumble and bang of the milk-truck.

Babbitt moaned; turned over; struggled back toward his dream.

Here, the author's voice is distinct without being as intrusive as Douglas Adams'. The Omniscient POV is flexible in this way. The author can choose just how much of a personal stamp and style to put on the voice.

Note: There is a style called "head hopping" that you'll sometimes run across. That's where the author switches from one POV to another within the same scene, without a space break. Like this:

Darla felt a thrill like never before when Jake touched her hand. Is this what true love was like? If so, she wanted more of it. To overflowing!

"I hope you'll come with me to the party," Jake said. He was surprised at his nervousness. What was it about this girl that set him on edge?

See what happened? What Darla thinks is not something Jake can perceive, so we are definitely within her POV. But the second paragraph gives us Jake's thoughts, so we can't be in Darla's head anymore. We've "hopped" over to Jake.

Most editors these days will call that a mistake. Technically, it's not. It's just a form of non-intrusive Omniscient POV. Omniscient means "all knowing," so the author can be wherever he or she wants to be, inside any head at any time.

Today, the Omniscient POV, especially the kind where the

author's voice is apparent, is not in fashion. Readers want to experience a story right along with the characters, to be taken on an emotional ride through a vicarious identification.

Which is not to say Omniscient cannot legitimately be employed. Large-scale epics, say in the historical or speculative fiction genres, may find an Omniscient narrative useful, at least for parts of the novel.

But even so, most authors today feel the best choice for a scene is to get into one character's head and heart, and stay there. An entire novel can be written from one character's POV. Or POV can shift between scenes. In either case, capturing the voice of the POV character (via the CAP Method) will render the voices unique and memorable.

Should You Use A Voiceless Voice?

Not every writer is interested in developing a distinctive voice for a novel. Isaac Asimov, the famous science fiction writer, purposely used a stripped-down, almost conversational style so he could write fast and just tell the story.

Nothing wrong with that. In fact, it has worked pretty well for James Patterson and his legion of co-writers. For example, in *Burn*, by Patterson and Michael Ledwidge, the descriptive passages are brief and functional. When the lead character, Michael Bennett, goes to his new assignment in Harlem, he describes the corner this way:

> There were sidewalk vendors and bustling clothing stores and lines of people in front of curbside food carts. There was also a lot of scaffolding and cranes from new construction and building renovations. I even saw a Times Square-style double-decker bus go by filled with wide-eyed tourists.

This is generic. The use of *There were* and *there was* and *a lot* is plain-vanilla writing. The strings of images make no attempt to connect the description to the inner life of the character or deepen the tone. It is merely to set up the scene, which is all action. That is Patterson's forté.

His readers don't seem to mind.

Maybe when you sell a million copies per book, you could be happy writing this way.

But why not go for the gold? Compare the above description with this opening from Mickey Spillane's *The Killing Man*:

> Some days hang over Manhattan like a huge pair of

unseen pincers, slowly squeezing the city until you can hardly breathe. A low growl of thunder echoed up the cavern of Fifth Avenue and I looked up to where the sky started at the seventy-first floor of the Empire State Building. I could smell the rain. It was like the kind that hung above the orderly piles of concrete until it was soaked with dust and debris and when it came down it wasn't rain at all, but the sweat of the city.

Now that is voice, friends. That is what makes a noir classic as opposed to transient fiction that is forgotten as soon as it's finished.

Spillane's prose is an example of the character (Mike Hammer) and the author coming together and putting the story on the page with a memorable style.

This is what makes great writing.

When you read Spillane, you know it.

When you read Michael Connelly, you know it.

When you read Raymond Chandler, you know it.

Nora Roberts has a voice for romance, and a voice for her futuristic noirs written as J. D. Robb.

Why not go for unforgettable?

In the next several chapters, I'm going to give you some other voice sparkers. Think of the CAP Method as the omelette with all the unique ingredients you've added through character and author symbiosis.

What follow are the spices.

The Joy Secret

Should writers worry about voice?

No, writers shouldn't worry about anything.

But they do.

They worry about finding an agent or a publisher. They worry about self-publishing and marketing.

Most of all, they worry that their stuff isn't good enough for the market or critics.

A writer should never write with worry or fear. When you're writing worried and thinking too much about it, you choke off voice.

The best writing comes when you put down words with a certain abandon.

In fact, you need to write with *joy*.

> "In the great story-tellers, there is a sort of self-enjoyment in the exercise of the sense of narrative; and this, by sheer contagion, communicates enjoyment to the reader. Perhaps it may be called (by analogy with the familiar phrase, "the joy of living") the joy of telling tales. The joy of telling tales which shines through Treasure Island is perhaps the main reason for the continued popularity of the story. The author is having such a good time in telling his tale that he gives us necessarily a good time in reading it." - Clayton Meeker Hamilton, *A Manual of the Art of Fiction* (1919)

I think Professor Hamilton nailed it. When an author is joyous in the writing, it pulses through the words. When you read a Ray Bradbury, for instance, you sense his joy. He was in love with words and his own imagination, and it showed.

"For the first thing a writer should be is—excited," writes Bradbury in *Zen in the Art of Writing*. "He should be a thing of fevers and enthusiasms. Without such vigor, he might as well be out picking peaches or digging ditches; God knows it'd be better for his health."

"Let her go!" says Brenda Ueland in *If You Want to Write*. "Be careless, reckless! Be a lion, be a pirate!"

You like to play those things when you were a kid, right? So play those things as a writer.

I recall a *Writer's Digest* fiction column by Lawrence Block, back in the 80s, and he was telling about being at a book signing with some other authors, one of whom was a guy named Stephen King. And Stephen King's line was longer by far than for any of the other guys.

Which got Larry to thinking, what was it about King's stuff? And he decided that it was this joy aspect. When you read Stephen King, you feel like you're reading an author who loves writing, loves making up tales to creep us out, enjoys the very act of setting words down on paper.

Because when you're joyful in the writing, the writing is fresher and fuller. Fuller of what? Of you. And that translates to the page and becomes that thing called Voice.

So the question is, how can you get more joy into your writing?

Here are some thoughts:

1. Stay excited about your story. If you're not jazzed about what you're writing, you can't be joyful about writing it. Dwight Swain, the great writing teacher, once said that the secret of excitement is to go deeper into your characters. So if your project starts feeling like drudgery, pause and give your character a secret, a trauma, a ghost from the past. Play around, and soon you'll get excited again.

2. Re-read something you loved. I find that if I read a passage by one of my favorite writers, I soon enough get excited about writing all over again and want to go back to my project.

3. Go on writing sprints. That's where you write so fast you don't let your brain assess what you put on the page. At all. Your goal is to over-write, just pour yourself out on the page, especially when you're writing about a character's emotions. Let your wild, writer's mind run free, and you'll see nuggets coming up to the surface. Edit later and use what you will.

4. First thing in the morning (or second thing, after making coffee) write for 5-10 minutes without stopping, letting the stuff that cooked in your mind during the night have some time in the sun.

5. Or try a writing prompt (there are several good books and websites that offer these) and write for five minutes.

Finally, when you start on your project, write like a house afire.

Later, you'll edit like an arson investigator.

But burn when you write, which is a function of joy.

Use some of that joy to explore your character more deeply. That's the subject of the following chapter.

The Emotion Factor

As authors, we want to weave a fictive dream, make it vivid, and stop doing things that jog readers out of the trance. That's one of the big reasons for studying the craft—learning to spot the "speed bumps" that jolt a reader, even a little bit, out of your dream.

Now, dreams are experienced emotionally and, only later, analyzed for meaning. It's the same with fiction. We want the readers to be emotionally engaged and, when the book is over, thinking what a great ride it was.

So emotion is a big key to going deeper.

Something I emphasize in my workshops are what I call *crosscurrents of emotion*. This occurs when readers are not only experiencing the surface emotion of a scene or character, but also other emotions that complicate things, even running against the emotion that is primary.

The nice thing about this is readers do not pause to analyze their emotions. They feel them, and the more going on, the better.

Crosscurrents of emotion are created in three ways.

1. Characters in Conflict

Let's say a boy and girl meet, they are attracted to one another. The boy is a vampire. He wants to kiss the girl but also suck her blood. You could write that scene just emphasizing the emotion of love. Or just the horror part. But if you have equally strong currents of bloodsucking lust and incipient romance, you get an almost instant emotional deepening.

So how do you get at some of these deeper emotions in your fiction?

First, dig deeper into the character to find unique, surprising colors.

Then add those colors to a scene, especially if they are cutting against the grain of the obvious.

Here are a few deepening exercises:

Chair Through the Window

Imagine that your lead character is in a nice living room with a big bay window. The window looks out on a lovely garden. There is a chair sitting by the piano. Your Lead picks up the chair and throws it through the window. Now ask yourself why. What would make your character do that? This surprising, even shocking action is motivated by something. Brainstorm what that is until you find the motivation that strikes you in the gut.

Closet Search

The police come to where your character lives. They have a search warrant. In your character's closet is one thing that she never wants anyone to see, ever. What is that thing? What does that tell you about her inner life? Brainstorm that item until you find something fresh and, more important, disturbing.

Good Cop / Bad Cop

Now your character is sitting under the hot lights in an old 1940s film noir. There is a tough, cigar-smoking police detective who is haranguing your character, trying to force her to admit something. What is she trying to hide? When you find out what it is, the thing that she does not want to reveal to anyone, have her fight back against the bad cop. She won't talk. But she is sweating under those lights. Then the good cop steps in and tells the bad cop to leave the room. He is warm and understanding and your character trusts him. Now she makes her confession. What does she tell this cop?

The Dickens

Go forward in time twenty years from the end of your novel. If you've done a Civil War novel, go to 1885. If you've done a sci-fi novel set in 3156, go to 3176. You are now going to play reporter and interview your Lead. If your Lead has died in the novel, talk to the ghost. This is called The Dickens because you are going to the future, like Scrooge did, and see what happens.

Now, sit down with your reporter's notepad and ask the Lead these questions:

• Why did you have to go through all that (the events of the novel)?

• What did you learn about yourself?

• What did you learn about life?

• If you could give a message to today's audience, what would it be?

• What would your life have been like had you *not* experienced the novel? Is that the sort of life you would have preferred?

The Dickens may be done at any time, but is one of the best exercises after you've read your first draft for the first time.

A Look in the Mirror

The best for last: This is where you go to the middle of your book and have your Lead metaphorically (though it can be literally, too) look at herself in the mirror and ask things like, *What kind of person am I? Who must I become to be whole? Why am I doing this to people?*

Or, if the book is primarily about physical action, reflect: *I am probably going to die. There are too many forces against me. I can't possibly survive!*

37

For me, this is the single most valuable structure tool in the entire shed. That's why I wrote a whole book about the mirror moment called *Write Your Novel From the Middle*.

2. Conflict in Readers

You can do things to create crosscurrents of emotion in the readers themselves. One of the most powerful ways to do this is to give a villain a sympathy factor. This is much more effective than the stereotypical, all-evil-all-the-time bad guy. Readers don't want to empathize with evil, and that's a good thing. But they also don't want to be manipulated. By giving them a fully rounded villain, you create emotions in conflict *inside the reader.*

The amazing thing is the readers won't dislike you for that. Instead, they will sense that the whole reading experience has done something to them on the inside. And you know what they'll do after that? Recommend your book to their friends! That's the secret to a career, ladies and gentlemen.

3. Tears in the Writer

Robert Frost said, "No tears in the writer, no tears in the reader." The meaning is obvious. Unless you, dear writer, are experiencing something emotionally as you write, your scene will have that much less "vibration" in it. Just as *joy* is evident when you are telling your tale well, so too is emotional vibrancy apparent.

Remember the opening of *Romancing the Stone?* Romance writer Joan Wilder (Kathleen Turner) has headphones on, pumping music, as she types the last scene of her WIP. And by the end of it, she's crying up a storm.

You need to experience some waterworks, too, writer. But also *any* strong emotion as you write a scene.

How do you get there? You place your characters in real conflict. You get inside the viewpoint character's head. You call upon your own life to experience what that character is experiencing (use the *psychological gesture* discussed earlier in this book).

Now, write that scene for all it's worth. *Overwrite* it, in fact. You can always pull back on the intensity level when you revise.

Get emotional!

Get the blood flowing.

More on that in the next chapter.

Get the Blood Flowing

It was Red Smith, not Ernest Hemingway, who said there was nothing to writing, you just sit down at the typewriter and bleed. (The writers of an HBO movie about Hemingway stole the line and put it in his mouth, which just goes to show you can plagiarize even when you're dead).

So one of the best ways to coax out voice is to get more blood pumping through your veins. Then, take that heat and translate it into your fiction.

Start the Flow

Write down the ten things you care about most in the world. People, issues, causes, whatever comes to your mind. These can be things you are positive or negative about. Someone's list might look like this:

My daughter
Learning
Oppressed religions
Justice
Equal opportunity
Dogs
Crime
Liars
Swindlers
Politicians

Now write a page under each topic, talking to yourself

about why you feel so strongly about it. Don't just go with the easy answers. Dig deep. Someone might write along these lines:

> Dogs:
> I care about dogs because I love them, always have. They're goodness and loyalty, unlike a lot of people. When I was seven we had a dog but he got hit by a car and it was horrible for me, I cried and cried, and my parents never got another one, and it was only after my divorce that I was able to take the risk to get another dog, Buckley, and he is the one who brought me back to life. I hate, hate, hate to see dogs mistreated, and I hate, hate, hate when certain breeds are raised by thugs to do harm, that's just like child abuse in my book. So does that explain it all? Maybe I care more about dogs than people right now, and that's not a good place to be, but if I had to choose between Buckley and my ex, it would be a no brainer.

You get the idea. Your blood is starting to flow as you write. You can feel it.

Now, take a step back and try to summarize, in one or two words, what that topic you just wrote about means to you. What summarizes your feelings?

Maybe in the dog example it would be Loyalty and Love. Or Healing.

Do that for each of the topics you write down in your original list.

You now have a list of keywords for the things you care about most.

Each time you set out to start a project, make one of those keywords the thing your Lead character cares about most. Set up your plot to test the Lead on that belief.

Your writing will have a vibrancy that comes from your own caring and passion.

Listen to Music

One of the best ways to get that flow going is by listening

to music. Specifically, music that is tied to the kind of mood you're after for a particular scene.

I like movie soundtracks for this. I have a collection of scores I've used to help get me in various moods.

Since I write mostly suspense, I rely on scores from movies by that master of suspense, Alfred Hitchcock. His great collaborator was Bernard Herrmann. *North by Northwest, Vertigo, Torn Curtain.*

On the more contemporary side I favor Carter Burwell's *Burn After Reading,* the Hans Zimmer *Sherlock Holmes* score, and John Ottman's *Gothika.*

When I want something heartfelt, I bring up two of the greatest scores of all time: *The Best Years of Our Lives* by Hugo Friedhofer, and Elmer Bernstein's score for *To Kill A Mockingbird.* Also, *October Sky* by Mark Isham and *Road to Perdition* by Thomas Newman.

Heroic? *The Big Country* by Jerome Moross and *Ben-Hur* by Miklós Rózsa.

Put together your own lists. Set your heart in motion, and write.

Voice will begin to happen naturally.

Write at Peak Energy Times

We all know when we're at our best. For some it's mornings, for others it's after most people are in bed.

And in between are peaks and valleys.

My own creative energy is best early, while it's still dark. I love that time. I get the coffee going and park myself at the keyboard, put on some rain sounds or the background noise of Coffitivity.com and go to work.

I can usually put in four hours straight of good, solid writing time (which includes short breaks every thirty minutes or so, just to stretch and deep breathe a little).

From about ten to noon I still experience some good energy for writing, then knock off for lunch.

From one to three is my "zombie time." I can't do much of anything then. I realize, of course, that I've already put in about six hours of work already. But even if I haven't done that much my body wants to be the walking dead in that zone.

So I fool it and take a power nap. Twenty minutes.

Then I pick and choose thirty-minute spots for more writing or editing if need be.

Get to know your own body rhythms in that way. Because voice comes best out of energetic writing.

The Power of Attitude

Give your POV characters attitude.

Real attitude. Because that will show up on the page.

This is especially important when you write in First Person POV. From the very first page we have got to hear a character who has some real heat going on, and is letting it come out.

Take a look at a few openings in First Person POV and listen to the 'tude:

> If you really want to hear about it, the first thing you'll probably want to know is where I was born, and what my lousy childhood was like, and how my parents were occupied and all before they had me, and all that David Copperfield kind of crap, but I don't feel like going into it, if you want to know the truth. - J. D. Salinger, *The Catcher in the Rye*

> When I was a little girl I used to dress Barbie up without underpants. On the outside, she'd look like the perfect lady. Tasteful plastic heels, tailored suit. But underneath, she was naked. I'm a bail enforcement agent now— also known as a fugitive apprehension agent, also known as a bounty hunter. I bring 'em back dead or alive. At least I try. And being a bail enforcement agent is a little like being bare-bottom Barbie. It's about having a secret. And it's about wearing a lot of bravado on the outside when you're really operating without underpants. - Janet Evanovich, *High Five*

> Late in the winter of my seventeenth year, my mother

decided I was depressed, presumably because I rarely left the house, spent quite a lot of time in bed, read the same book over and over, ate infrequently, and devoted quite a bit of my abundant free time to thinking about death.

Whenever you read a cancer booklet or website or whatever, they always list depression among the side effects of cancer. Depression is a side effect of dying. (Cancer is also a side effect of dying. Almost everything is, really.) But my mom believed I required treatment, so she took me to see my Regular Doctor Jim, who agreed that I was veritably swimming in a paralyzing and totally clinical depression, and that therefore my meds should be adjusted and also I should attend a weekly Support Group.

This Support Group featured a rotating cast of characters in various states of tumor-driven unwellness. Why did the cast rotate? A side effect of dying. - John Green, *The Fault in Our Stars*

Notice, however, that you can work the same attitude voice in Third Person as well. It makes the narrative sound as if it is coming right from the character's own thoughts.

Stick left his bourbon and went to the men's room. He was tired of hearing guys talk, guys wanting you to believe they were street, guys saying MAN all the time. He shouldn't have called Rainy. Well, maybe call him and have a drink, but he shouldn't have promised him anything. Stick washed his hands with the fragrant pink soap that came out of the dispenser, washed them good and stared into the clear mirror at his features. Pale, solemn. Who was that? Like looking at someone else. Back in another life before Jackson he could narrow his eyes at his reflection—hard-boned but not bad looking—and say, "That's it? That's all you got?" - Elmore Leonard, *Stick*

This next clip is from *Natural Born Charmer* by Susan Elizabeth Phillips. Her character Blue finds herself suddenly without funds and on the run. When her world collides with a bored and famous pro football player, she hitches a ride and goes to work for him and keeps him company. They couldn't be more different, but obviously one thing leads to another.

> It wasn't every day a guy saw a headless beaver march-ing down the side of a road, not even in Dean Robillard's larger-than-life world. "Son of a . . ." Dean slammed on the brakes of his brand-new Aston Martin Vanquis and pulled over in front of her.
>
> The beaver marched right past, her big flat tail bounc-ing in the gravel, and her small, sharp nose stuck up in the air. Way up. The beaver looked highly pissed.
>
> She was definitely a girl beaver because her beaver head was missing, revealing sweaty, dark hair pulled into a short, scraggly ponytail. He'd been praying for a little dis-traction from his own depressing company, so he threw open the door and stepped out onto the shoulder of the Colorado road. His newest pair of Dolce and Gabanna boots emerged first, followed by the rest of him, all six feet three inches of steely muscle, razor-sharp reflexes, and unsurpassed gorgeousness . . . or at least that's what his press agent liked to say. Still, it was pretty much true, although Dean didn't have nearly as much personal vanity as he let people believe. But emphasizing the superficial was a good way to keep people from getting any closer than he wanted them to be.
>
> "Uh, ma'am . . . You need some help?"
>
> Her paws didn't break rhythm. "You got a gun?"
>
> "Not with me."
>
> "Then I've got no use for you."

How do you form your character's attitude?

Go to your Voice Journal and start playing tough psychol-ogist with your character. Prompt him with questions and don't let him off the hook easily.

> *What do you think about women in the military?*
> I don't think about it, because it makes me mad.

Why does it make you mad?

You trying to be funny? Chicks with guns?

Explain.

What's to explain? You ever seen a woman drive a car? You want to put a rifle in their hands in combat? Remind me not to be your lead character anymore.

You have no choice.

We'll see about that.

You seem to have a lot of hostility toward women. Tell me why.

I don't have to tell you anything.

I'm going to make you, one way or another. Tell me about your mother.

Nah…

Tell me!

All right! She was hell on wheels, you want to know the truth. Drank a fifth of Canadian Club every night and drove around the neighborhood. Sometimes with me in the car!

We'll let the rest of the above session remain confidential. But you see the point. Dig deep and you'll find attitude, and when you find attitude you find voice.

Metaphors, Similes, and Word Pictures

Advanced fiction technique takes note of three types of colorful language:

1. Metaphors
2. Similes
3. Word pictures

There are subtle differences, and knowing what those are will help you bring variety to your writing.

A *metaphor* directly connects an image, word or phrase to something, in order to describe it. *It's a ghost of a moon tonight.*

A *simile* also connects, but does so with the word *like* or *as. The moon is like a ghost tonight.*

In an amusing article some time ago, a high-school teacher listed some of her students' first attempts at metaphor. One of them wrote:

He was as tall as a six-foot, three-inch tree.

Technically, that's a simile. Can you see why? Because of the word *as.*

The metaphor would be:

He was a tree of a man, six-three at least.

Another student wrote:

John and Mary had never met. They were like two hummingbirds, who had also never met.

Another simile (note the word *like*). To make it a metaphor:

> My friends John and Mary, a couple of hummingbirds in love, kept kissing each other in the elevator.

Raymond Chandler uses a simile to describe Philip Marlowe's first look at Moose Malloy in *Farewell, My Lovely*.

> A man was looking up at the sign too. He was looking up at the dusty windows with a sort of ecstatic fixity of expression, like a hunky immigrant catching his first sight of the Statue of Liberty.

Note the word *like* in there. That makes it a smile. Now look at the next line:

> He was a big man but not more than six feet five inches tall and not wider than a beer truck.

Chandler doesn't write that Moose was a beer truck of a man, or *like* a beer truck. It's simply his choice of words that makes the picture vivid.

I would call this a word picture. It's how an author chooses to describe something, the words used, the image created, the feeling evoked.

Here are a couple of examples of word pictures. Note they are more than mere description or listing of details:

> The sun that brief December day shone weakly through the west-facing window of Garrett Kingsley's office. It made a thin yellow oblong splash on his Persian carpet and gave up. (Robert B. Parker, *Pale Kings and Princes*)

> She sat up slowly, looked in turn at each of us, and her dark eyes were like twin entrances to two deep caves. Nothing lived in those caves. Maybe something had, once upon a time. There were piles of picked bones back in

there, some scribbling on the walls, and some gray ash where the fires had been. (John D. MacDonald, *Darker Than Amber*)

Novelist Tom Robbins is a wild, comic, head-expanding writer of crazy stories that are as much about voice as narrative. He is a master of simile and metaphor. One might venture to say he is the high priest of pictorial language, like an Aztec shaman lifting the feathers of rare and colorful birds then scattering them to the winds to fall softly before the eyes of hungry warriors.

Or something like that.

Here is a clip from his novel, *Jitterbug Perfume:*

The building in which this particular studio apartment donned its false beret was built during the Great Depression. In Seattle there are many such buildings, anointing their bricks in the rain on densely populated hillsides between Lake Washington and Elliott Bay. Architecturally, its plain façade and straight lines echoed the gown Eleanor Roosevelt wore to the inaugural ball, while its interior walls still reproduced faithfully the hues of the split pea much dished up in hundreds of soup kitchens. Over the years, the building had been so lived in that it had acquired a life of its own. Every toilet bowl gurgled like an Italian tenor with a mouthful of Lavoris, and the refrigerators made noises at night like buffalo grazing.

I crack up every time I read this. No other writer could compare a building to Eleanor Roosevelt's gown *and* split pea much in the same sentence. And I can just hear those toilet bowls and refrigerators.

Get in the habit of collecting examples of picturesque writing. Here are a few more from my collection:

From *Vengeance is Mine by* Mickey Spillane:

I put my arms around her, running my fingers through the sleek midnight of her hair.

From *Sacrifice* by Andrew Vachss (Burke, his anti-hero, is posing as a blind man):

> Humans passed around me, a stream breaking over a rock.
>
> Sheba settled into her task. An old wolf-shepherd, mostly gray, soft eyes watchful under white eyebrows. She had a warrior's heart and an undertaker's patience.

From the Dennis Lehane story "The Drop":

> Nadia was small. A bumpy red rope of a scar ran across the base of her throat like the smile of a drunk circus clown. She had a tiny moon of a face, savaged by pockmarks, and small, heart-pendant eyes. Shoulders that didn't cut so much as dissolve at the arms. Elbows like flattened beer cans. A yellow bob of hair curled on either side of her face.

Expanding Your Range

To grow in the use of metaphors, similes, and word pictures, *exercise the visual part of your imagination.* Here are a few ways to do that.

1. Open a dictionary at random and select the first noun you see.

2. Describe that thing four ways: sight, touch, smell, sound.

3. Make a list of ten other things that noun is like.

4. If you were describing this thing to a Martian who had never seen one, how would you do it?

5. Write a short scene where the Lead character in your current work-in-progress is in a state of high emotion, and

notices the noun. How would she describe it at that moment in time?

6. Mash up clichés. When your mind hands you a cliché, don't avoid it. Write it down and then play around with it. Can you change it up? Freshen it? Find another way to say it? In one of his stories Harlan Ellison described a character as looking like "a million bucks tax free."

The Page-Long Sentence

You are not Proust. Do not write long sentences. If they come into your head, write them, but then break them down. - Umberto Eco

Good advice there, Umberto, at least as far as the finished draft is concerned. But I'm going to make a case here for the *page-long* sentence during the writing of the first draft. It's a technique for squeezing character voice out of any emotional moment.

The technique is simple. When you come to a place of high emotion in a scene, pause and write a single, run-on sentence of at least 200 words. The sentence is the inner emotional response of the character. It is free-form. It concentrates only on that moment in time.

The sentence can be—in fact, should be—unstructured, wild, changing directions whenever your mind wants to go to a different spot.

You'll find this technique fun—joyful—as well as useful. Inevitably you will find one gem, and probably more, which you can incorporate into the final version of the scene.

In some cases, you might even decide to use the whole thing, re-worked a bit. It's powerful when that happens. It's voice on steroids.

Let me give you a couple of examples from published novels.

From *The Subterraneans* by Jack Kerouac:

So there we were at the Red Drum, a tableful of beers a few that is and all the gangs cutting in and out, paying a dollar quarter at the door, the little hip-pretending weasel there taking tickets, Paddy Cordavan floating in as prophesied (a big tall blond brakeman type subterranean from Eastern Washington cowboy-looking in jeans coming in to a wild generation party all smoky and mad and I yelled "Paddy Cordavan?" and "Yeah?" and he'd come over)—all sitting together, interesting groups and various tables, Julien, Roxanne (a woman of 25 prophesying the future style of America with short almost crewcut but with curls black snaky hair, snaky walk, pal pale junky anemic face and we say junky when once Dostoevski would have said what? if not ascetic or saintly? But not in the least? But the cold pale booster face of the cold blue girl and wearing a man's white shirt but with the cuffs undone untied at the buttons so I remember her leaning over talking to someone after having slinked across the floor with flowing propelled shoulders, bending to talk with her hand holding a short butt and the neat little flick she was giving it to knock ashes but repeatedly with long long fingernails an inch long and also orient and snake-like)—groups of all kinds and Ross Wallenstein, the crowd, and up on the stand Bird Parker with solemn eyes who'd been busted fairly recently and had now returned to a kind of bop dead Frisco but had just discovered or been told about the Red Drum, the great new generation gang wailing and gathering there...

And this one sentence goes on for another four pages! This is the Kerouac of the butcher-paper-in-the-typewriter-and-Benzedrine style of writing, which I can't recommend (the Benzedrine part, at least), but is instructive for us.

Two more examples:

Ask the Dust
John Fante
1939
(Technically, this is two sentences, but the cadence is what I'm after)

Los Angeles, give me some of you! Los Angeles come to me the way I came to you, my feet over your streets, you pretty town I loved you so much, you sad flower in the sand, you pretty town. A day and another day and the day before, and the library with the big boys in the shelves, old Dreiser, old Mencken, all the boys down there, and I went to see them, Hya Dreiser, Hya Mencken, Hya, hya: there's a place for me, too, and it begins with B, in the B shelf. Arturo Bandini, make way for Arturo Bandini, his slot for his book, and I sat at the table and just looked at the place where my book would be, right there close to Arnold Bennett, not much that Arnold Bennett, but I'd be there to sort of bolster up the B's, old Arturo Bandini, one of the boys, until some girl came along, some scent of perfume through the fiction room, some click of high heels to break up the monotony of my fame. Gala day, gala dream!

I'm not sure any writer of any era in any book has captured the yearning of a young writer so well.

I Should Have Stayed Home
Horace McCoy
1938

All Dorothy's fault, I thought, cursing her in my mind with all the dirty words I could think of, all the filthy ones I could remember the kids in my old gang used to yell at white women as they passed through the neighborhood on their way to work in the whore houses, these are what you are, Dorothy, turning off Vine onto the boulevard, feeling awful and alone, even worse than that time my dog was killed by the Dixie Flyer, but telling myself in a very faint voice that even like this I was better off than the fellows I grew up with back in Georgia who were married and had kids and regular jobs and regular salaries and were doing the same old thing in the same old way and would go on doing it forever.

Now it's your turn.

Go into your manuscript and find the scene where the hottest emotion is being played out. It may be a scene of conflict, or it may be a place where your character makes some discovery, or is hit with the worst news, or thinks all is hopeless.

Pick a moment. Write a page-long sentence about that moment.

Now forget about that sentence for at least two hours.

Come back to it and read it over, highlighting the words and phrases that jump out at you. Add to it if you like.

Pick the good stuff and work it into the scene.

Wow.

That's what you'll be saying. And so will your readers.

Poetry in Voice

John D. MacDonald, a great noir stylist, used to go for what he called "unobtrusive poetry" in his style.

So another way to expand your language possibilities in the use of voice is to read poetry every so often, and let the language sink in. Try writing poetry, too. Don't worry if it's bad. It most likely will be bad.

Just make yourself write outside your comfort zone.

Lawrence Ferlinghetti, one of the leading Beat poets, wrote a poem I love called *Dog*. Here's part of it. It was meant to be read aloud, with cool jazz in the background.

> The dog trots freely in the street
> And sees reality
> And the things he sees
> Are bigger than himself
> And the things he sees
> Are his reality
> Drunks in doorways
> Moons on trees
> The dog trots free thru the street
> And the things he sees
> Are smaller than himself
> Fish on newsprint
> Ants in holes
> Chickens in Chinatown windows
> Their heads a block away
> The dog trots freely in the street...

Write a poem of short lines. Don't worry about rhyme, just

let the words come out like a jazz riff. Here are some opening lines for a poem. You finish them:

I ate my keyboard and I'm still hungry

Last night I saw Hemingway in a dream

In Turkey, the soup is cold

Now, here is a very different kind of poem, one of the most famous in our language—*Leaves of Grass* by Walt Whitman (all grammar and style choices are the poet's):

> Listener up there! what have you to confide to me?
> Look in my face while I snuff the sidle of evening,
> (Talk honestly, no one else hears you, and I stay only a minute longer.)

> Do I contradict myself?
> Very well then I contradict myself,
> (I am large, I contain multitudes.)

> I concentrate toward them that are nigh, I wait on the door-slab.

> Who has done his day's work? who will soonest be through with his supper?
> Who wishes to walk with me?

> Will you speak before I am gone? will you prove already too late?

Try writing a poem with lines like that. Yes, you might feel silly. But guess what? Doing silly things is also good for the writer. And no one ever has to see these poems.

Ray Bradbury used to read a little poetry every day.

It's just one more way to get more sounds in your brain so you can lend them to your characters.

Learning to Vary Voice

The best writers, in my humble opinion, have the ability to vary the voice on the page according to the needs of the story.

Now, some writers spend entire careers working on one genre of book, even one series. Lee Child is not interested in straying from Jack Reacher. I'd say he's got a handle on that voice by now.

Dennis Lehane, on the other hand, has written genre crime novels, literary crime novels, and even strayed into historical territory. In each of these books he has changed the voice in masterful ways.

For example, here's a clip from Lehane's *Darkness, Take My Hand,* an early genre novel featuring series characters Patrick Kenzie and Angela Gennaro:

> Angie and I were up in our belfry office trying to fix the air conditioner when Eric Gault called.
>
> Usually in the middle of a New England October, a broken air conditioner wouldn't be a problem. A broken heater would. But it wasn't turning out to be a normal autumn. At two in the afternoon, the temperature hung in the mid-seventies and the window screens still carried the damp, baked odor of summer.
>
> "Maybe we should call someone," Angie said.
>
> I thumped the window unit on the side with my palm, turned it on again. Nothing.
>
> "I bet it's the belt," I said.

Notice the short sentence and paragraph structure, the clipped dialogue.

Now look at the style of Lehane's breakout novel, *Mystic River*, which reaches for a more literary style:

> Jimmy's mother sat down beside him on the curb, and Dave stepped away from the window. Jimmy's mother was a small, thin woman with the palest hair. For someone so thin, she moved as if she carried stacks of brick on each shoulder, and she sighed a lot and in such a way that Jimmy wasn't positive she knew the sound was coming out of her. He would look at pictures of her that had been taken before she'd become pregnant with him, and she looked a lot less thin and so much younger, like a teenage girl (which, when he did the math, was exactly what she'd been). Her face was rounder in the pictures, with no lines by the eyes or on the forehead, and she had this beautiful, full smile that seemed just slightly frightened, or maybe curious, Jimmy could never tell for sure. His father had told him a thousand times that Jimmy had almost killed her coming out, that she'd bled and bled until the doctors worried she might never stop bleeding. It had wiped her out, his father had said. And, of course, there would be no more babies. No one wanted to go through that again.

The difference is obvious. The above clip is one paragraph filled with compound sentences (and even a parenthetical). It takes its time with description and exposition.

Finally, let's look at Lehane's long historical novel, *The Given Day*. In this scene Babe Ruth, just starting out on his fabulous career in 1918, is waiting at a train stop when he hears the sound of baseball from across the tracks.

> He crossed the field alone and unnoticed and he heard the sounds of the ball game grow closer—the singsong of catcalls, the rough scuff of feet chasing down a ball in the grass, the wet-slap thump of a ball sent to its death in an outfielder's glove. He went through the trees and removed

his coat in the heat, and when he stepped out of the grove they were changing sides, men running in toward a patch of dirt along the first base line while another group ran out from a patch by third.

Colored men.

He stood where he was and nodded at the center fielder trotting out to take his spot a few yards from him, and the center fielder gave him a curt nod back and then appeared to scan the trees to see if they planned on giving birth to any more white men today. Then he turned his back to Babe and bent at the waist and placed his hand and glove on his knees. He was a big buck, as broad-shouldered as the Babe, though not as heavy in the middle...

Here's what I want you to notice about this passage. The voice is the narrator's, but it is reflective of Babe Ruth in that historical moment. A modern narrator in a non-fiction book would describe the baseball players as African-American. But Babe Ruth would not have used that term. *Colored* and *buck* were very much in use in 1918. Those are the terms Ruth would have used.

The symbiosis of character, history, and author (Lehane) are woven seamlessly into the narrative.

Another reason to learn to vary your voice is that we are living in a new "pulp" age. That's what I call the self-publishing revolution. Scores of writers are making terrific incomes writing and publishing at a rapid pace.

That's how the old pulp writers had to do it. At a penny a word, they needed to be prolific to make ends meet, especially during the Depression.

One of the best of those was Robert E. Howard (1906-1936). In his short life and career Howard (best known as the creator of Conan the Barbarian) cranked out hundreds of stories in a variety of genres. Take a look at the different voices from this one author:

Conan the Barbarian stories:

It was Valeria who exclaimed, but they both started violently, and Conan wheeled like a cat, his great sword flashing into his hand. Back in the forest had burst forth an appalling medley of screams—the screams of horses in terror and agony. Mingled with their screams there came the snap of splintering bones. "Lions are slaying the horses!" cried Valeria.

"Lions, nothing!" snorted Conan, his eyes blazing. "Did you hear a lion roar? Neither did I! Listen to those bones snap—not even a lion could make that much noise killing a horse." (Red Nails)

Steve Costigan boxing stories:

The minute I seen the man they'd picked to referee the fight between me and Red McCoy, I didn't like his looks. His name was Jack Ridley and he was first mate aboard the Castleton, one of them lines which acts very high tone, making their officers wear uniforms. Bah! The first cap'n I ever sailed with never wore nothing at sea but a pair of old breeches, a ragged undershirt and a month's growth of whiskers. He used to say uniforms was all right for navy admirals and bell-hops but they was a superflooity anywheres else.

Well, this Ridley was a young fellow, slim and straight as a spar, with cold eyes and a abrupt manner. (Alleys of Peril)

Historical stories:

The roar of battle had died away; the sun hung like a ball of crimson gold on the western hills. Across the trampled field of battle no squadrons thundered, no war-cry reverberated. Only the shrieks of the wounded and the moans of the dying rose to the circling vultures whose black wings swept closer and closer until they brushed the pallid faces in their flight.

On his rangy stallion, in a hillside thicket, Ak Boga the Tatar watched, as he had watched since dawn, when the mailed hosts of the Franks, with their forest of lances and flaming pennons, had moved out on the plains of Nicopolis to meet the grim hordes of Bayazid. (Lord of Samarcand)

Fantasy stories:

I instantly realized that the being, hostile or not, was a formidable figure. He fairly emanated strength—hard, raw, brutal power. There was not an ounce of surplus flesh on him. His frame was massive, with heavy bones. His hairy skin rippled with muscles that looked iron-hard. Yet it was not altogether his body that spoke of dangerous power. His look, his carriage, his whole manner reflected a terrible physical might backed by a cruel and implacable mind. As I met the blaze of his bloodshot eyes, I felt a wave of corresponding anger. The stranger's attitude was arrogant and provocative beyond description. I felt my muscles tense and harden instinctively. (Almuric)

Westerns:

I been accused of prejudice agen the town of Red Cougar, on account of my habit of avoiding it if I have to ride fifty miles outen my way to keep from going through there. I denies the slander. It ain't no more prejudiced for me to ride around Red Cougar than it is for a lobo to keep his paw out of a jump-trap. My experiences in that there lair of iniquity is painful to recall. I was a stranger and took in. I was a sheep for the fleecing, and if some of the fleecers got their fingers catched in the shears, it was their own fault. (Evil Deeds at Red Cougar)

Whatever your aim as a writer, it is good practice to stretch and grow in the area of voice. It will only improve your writing because, as the subtitle of this book suggests, it is truly the secret power.

Variance Exercise:

1. Take your current work-in-progress (WIP) and place your Lead character in a room, alone.

2. Describe the room.

3. Now, change the genre of this scene four times. Let's say you're writing steampunk. You might choose:
    Noir
    Romance
    Thriller
    Science Fiction

4. Describe the room again, in each of the four different genres.

5. Vary between First Person POV and Third Person POV in your descriptions.

This will yield eight different descriptive passages. Tweak them until each has a distinct voice.

Minimalism and Voice

There is a type of voice that might seem, at first glance, to be antithetical to the whole concept. That's the literary school known as minimalism. Flowering within MFA programs in the 80s and 90s, minimalism held out for the least possible intrusion of style into fiction. The idea is to create reality on the page that draws the reader into immediate experience.

The style was popularized by Ernest Hemingway, who announced his intention to write one "true sentence" after another. He was hugely influential. Many (mostly male) authors tried to imitate him, and always fell short of the original. Hemingway-style writing looks easy, but is in fact difficult to pull off. (This is why there is a popular Imitation Hemingway Contest every year. I was a semi-finalist one year, before returning to literary obscurity).

Minimalism caught on with the hard-boiled school of the 1920s and 1930s, led by Dashiell Hammett and James M. Cain.

In the 1970s, minimalism became a literary style popularized by writers such as Raymond Carver, with whom I had the privilege to study in college.

Here is a bit from Hemingway's *For Whom the Bell Tolls:*

> As Robert Jordan buttoned the flap of his pocket and then lay flat behind the pine trunk, looking out from behind it, Anselmo put his hand on his elbow and pointed with one finger.
>
> In the sentry box that faced toward them up the road, the sentry was sitting holding his rifle, the bayonet fixed, between his knees. He was smoking a cigarette and he wore a knitted cap and blanket style cape. At fifty yards, you

could not see anything about his face. Robert Jordan put up his field glasses, shading the lenses carefully with his cupped hands even though there was now no sun to make a glint, and there was the rail of the bridge as clear as though you could reach out and touch it and there was the face of the sentry so clear he could see the sunken cheeks the ash on the cigarette and the greasy shine of the bayonet. It was a peasant's face, the cheeks hollow under the high cheekbones, the beard stubbled, the eyes shaded by the heavy brows, big hands holding the rifle, heavy boots showing beneath the folds of the blanket cape. There was a worn, blackened leather wine bottle on the wall of the sentry box, there were some newspapers and there was no telephone.

The specificity of detail here is setting up the reader to feel the mounting tension. The bayonet is mentioned twice, once at a distance and once close up. The reader is getting these impressions right along with the POV character, Robert Jordan.

Raymond Carver was considered a late 20th century master of the minimalist style. In his workshop, one of the stories we were assigned to read was his "Will You Please Be Quiet, Please?" Below is a clip from that story:

In eight years they had two children, Dorothea and Robert, who were now five and four years old. A few months after Robert, Marian had accepted at mid-term a part-time position as a French and English teacher at Harris Junior College, at the edge of town. The position has become full-time and permanent that next fall, and Ralph had stayed on, happily, at the high school. In the time they had been married, they had had only one serious distur-bance, and that was long ago: two years ago that winter to be exact. It was something they had never talked about since it happened, but, try as he might, Ralph couldn't help thinking about it sometimes. On occasion, and then when he was least prepared, the whole ghastly scene leaped into his mind. Looked at rationally and in its proper, historical perspective, it seemed impossible and monstrous; an event of such personal magnitude for Ralph that he still couldn't entirely accept it as something that had once happened to Marian and himself: he had taken it into his head one night at a party that Marian had betrayed him with Mitchell Anderson, a friend. In a fit of uncontrollable rage, he had struck Marian with his fist, knocking her sideways against the kitchen table and onto the floor.

Carver did not adorn his style. He let the words convey the action so the emotion was felt by the reader directly. His genius was in selecting just the right details to illuminate a scene and character psychology. It's a difficult style to master, but when it is done well it has a powerful impact.

To further your appreciation of minimalism, let me recommend the following:

The Maltese Falcon by Dashiell Hammett
The Postman Always Rings Twice by James M. Cain
The Short Stories of Ernest Hemingway

Voice in Description

Description is where voice has a chance to shine. You can do two things simultaneously: tell us more about who the character is, and deepen the emotion of the scene for the reader.

Here's what I mean. Below is a paragraph of generic description taken from my observations of Broadway in downtown Los Angeles:

> Sky blue, sun hot. Traffic fairly heavy. a lot of pedestrian activity. Salsa music being piped loudly from one of the stores selling T-shirts and hats along the street. A mother holding an unruly male child by the hand, trying to get him to cooperate in walking along. They pass a woman wearing the rich, pink colored flowing clothes of India.

Now, depending upon the mood I want to create and the inner life of my character at a certain moment, I can render these details in various ways. Here's one impression:

> I came out onto Broadway and the sun blasted my face. I almost had to play hopscotch with a car racing by. Instead, I gave it a good parting shot with my right arm and middle finger. My head was starting to ache, and the salsa music polluting my ears didn't help. When I walked past a woman holding a brat I thought my day was complete. But a woman looking like a bad stick of candy swept by me, and I wondered for a moment if I was in some alien world.

Compare that to this:

> She felt the invigorating warmth of the sun as she stepped out onto Broadway. The hum of activity was like a shot of adrenaline. People in cars going places, people on the street walking, heading in one direction or another, not standing still. Even the complaining boy with his mother was a sign of hope. He had passion, and that would get him somewhere someday, sure, just like she was going to make it, finally, in the City of Angels.
>
> Mary smiled and nodded at the woman in the beautiful salwar.

Try this:

1. Write out a detailed description of one of your favorite spots.

2. Write out the description from the POV of a character who hates the place.

3. Write out a description from the POV of someone who is in love.

4. Now, go into your WIP and look for descriptive passages. Heat them up with the emotion that your POV character feels. If you've already done that, turn up the heat ten percent.

Location Work

I always like to go to the locations I'm going to write about. I take lots of pictures and notes. The first step in getting to a descriptive voice is to be accurate about what you observe.

Here is a checklist of what I look for. Feel free to replicate it and use it in your own research. Just be sure to be as specific as possible when filling it out.

Name of location
Date of visit
Weather conditions
Main sights
Names and types of establishments
Food and drink
Smells
Sounds
People notes:
Ethnicity
Clothing
Facial expressions
Possible backstory (I always like to do a little imaginative work here, fleshing out possible supporting characters)
Eavesdropping notes:
Regionalisms (ways of speaking)
Subject matter
Interview notes (formal or informal conversations with locals)
Chamber of Commerce or Visitor Center notes:
History
Famous or infamous events
Brochures
Tourist attractions

Now filter these notes through the character, via the CAP Method. No more generic description or "info dumps." Just voice on display.

Like this description of San Francisco, written by John D. MacDonald, via his series character, Travis McGee:

San Francisco is the most depressing city in America. The come-latelys might not think so. They may be enchanted by the steep streets of Nob and Russian and Telegraph, by the sea mystery of the Bridge over to redwood country on a foggy night, by the urban compartmentalization of Chinese, Spanish, Greek, Japanese, by the smartness of the women and the city's iron clutch on culture. It might look just fine to the new ones.

But there are too many of us who used to love her. She was like a wild classy kook of a gal, one of those rain-walkers, laughing gray eyes, tousle of dark hair—sea misty, a lithe and lively lady, who could laugh at you or with you, and at herself when needs be. A sayer of strange and lovely things. A girl to be in love with, with love like a heady magic.

But she had lost it, boy. She used to give it away, and now she sells it to the tourists. She imitates herself. Her figure has thickened. The things she says now are mechanical and memorized. She overcharges for cynical services. (*The Quick Red Fox*)

Voice in Non-Fiction

Non-fiction writers have voices, too.

They can be witty, scholarly, light, heavy, informative, snarky, clear ... or if they're not careful, obtuse.

It all depends on the goal of the non-fiction piece.

Most of the time someone writes non-fiction to communicate an idea or illuminate a topic. Thus, the first order of business is to be *clear*.

A Facebook ditty that made the rounds may be apocryphal, but illustrates the point. A student asked his teacher why the research paper he submitted received such a low grade. The teacher responded:

> Actually, you didn't turn in a research paper. You turned in a random assemblage of sentences. In fact, the sentences you apparently kidnapped in the dead of night and forced into this violent and arbitrary plan of yours clearly seemed to be placed on the pages against their will. Reading your paper was like watching unfamiliar, uncomfortable people interacting at a cocktail party that no one wanted to attend in the first place. You didn't submit a research paper. You submitted a hostage situation.

Don't write hostage situations.

Be clear.

Clarity comes from knowing exactly what you want to say in a sentence, and getting "clutter" out of the way of the meaning.

William Zinsser, the author of the classic book on non-fiction, *On Writing Well,* said this:

> Clutter is the disease of American writing. We are a society strangling in unnecessary words, circular constructions, pompous frills and meaningless jargon ... [T]he secret of good writing is to strip every sentence to its cleanest components. Every word that serves no function, every long word that could be a short word, every adverb that carries the same meaning that's already in the verb, every passive construction that leaves the reader unsure of who is doing what—these are the thousand and one adulterants that weaken the strength of a sentence.

Unless your purpose is to make your voice the star of the piece, aim first for clarity.

Strive for simple sentences that carry only one thought.

Later, if you want to move into more performance-style non-fiction, you'll be starting with the right foundation.

Performance Voice

If the voice is wholly or in part performance—where the book is as much about the author as it is about the subject—then you seek to press everything through your view of the subject.

As in the Gonzo school of writing.

Gonzo is a type of writing popularized by Hunter S. Thompson, the wild man reporter for such journals as *Rolling Stone.* It does not have one definition, but primarily it is a voice thing. The author is part of the story. It is less important to be objectively accurate than to recreate a feeling, a mood, an experience.

Take a look at this excerpt from Thompson's *Fear and Loathing in Las Vegas* (1971):

> We were somewhere around Barstow on the edge of the desert when the drugs began to take hold.

Notice the author is inside the events from the get go. Thompson is not just a reporter or observer. He's a player. The story will be about him as much as it is about his assignment, which he describes as follows:

> The sporting editors had also given me $300 in cash, most of which was already spent on extremely dangerous drugs. The trunk of the car looked like a mobile police narcotics lab. We had two bags of grass, seventy-five pellets of mescaline, five sheets of high-powered blotter acid, a salt shaker half full of cocaine, and a whole galaxy of multi-colored uppers, downers, screamers, laughers and also a quart of tequila, a quart of rum, a case of Budweiser, a pint of raw ether and two dozen amyls....
>
> Not that we needed all that for the trip, but once you get locked into a serious drug-collection, the tendency is to push it as far as you can.

Whatever your take on the message of Mr. Thompson, you cannot deny that there is a distinct, honest, and wild voice.

Where did Gonzo writing come from? While the term may have originated with (or about) Hunter S. Thompson, something very much like it had been practiced by the writers known as the Beats. This movement began in America in the 1950s. It was largely a reaction against literary conventions. The writers were not so interested in, say, plot. They were interested in capturing and sharing experience.

In the 1960s, a young journalist named Tom Wolfe was trying to write a traditional article about car culture in Southern California. It wasn't working for him. He just had a bunch of notes, and finally wrote a long letter to his editor, along with the notes.

The editor ran this material pretty much as is, and the "new journalism" was born.

Sometimes, voice in non-fiction is simply getting out of the way and letting the event tell itself. As in this, from *Hollywood Days, Hollywood Nights* by Ben Stein:

One day she came over when I was talking to my parents in Washington, D.C. When I got off the phone, I told her whom I had been talking to and where they lived.

"Oh, in Washington. Where it rains all the time," she exclaimed.

"No, in Washington, D.C. You're thinking of Washington State."

"What's the difference?" Stacey asked cheerfully.

"One is the capital of the United States," I said. "The other is a state in the Pacific Northwest."

"Really?" Stacey said. "Which is which?"

When it comes to non-fiction, my overall advice is: first be clear, then be clever. Communicate, then entertain.

And then revise and revise until your purpose is realized.

Some Non-Fiction Writing Tips

My favorite book on non-fiction is Zinsser's *On Writing Well*.

It's also a good idea to have a usage manual close for easy reference. I like *Write Right!* by Jan Venolia.

Over the years I've picked up a few tips I try to keep in mind in my non-fiction:

When in doubt, use a period

An old newspaper editor once said, "The period is the greatest grammatical tool known to man. Use it!" Vary the length of your sentences for different rhythms, but set your default to the simple sentence.

Organize your thoughts with a mind map

Before you write non-fiction, use a mind map to come up with ideas and organize your thoughts. The mind map is random thoughts written on a blank piece of paper or computer document (I like to use a pen and paper for maximum freedom). I put circles around the thoughts and write down any sub-thoughts that occur to me. I connect thoughts with lines. Only later do I organize them by assigning numbers to the thoughts.

You can mind map a whole book, or one chapter/section. Here's what one of my mind maps looked like for a chapter in another book:

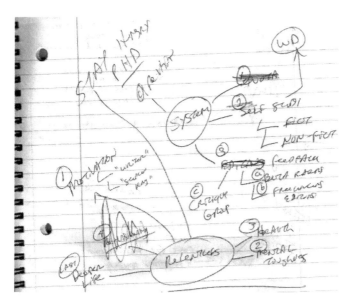

Go on an adverb hunt

Learn to identify adverbs and be relentless in taking them out. I'm not saying never to use an adverb. I certainly do (see?) when I feel it helps. But going on an *-ly* search of your document will give you opportunities to use strong active verbs instead.

If you're not sure what an adverb is, you'll benefit from some study. Here's a good article to start with:

http://www.quickanddirtytips.com/education/grammar/how-to-eliminate-adverbs

Avoid clichés like a heat rash

Every year it seems a fresh crop of clichés is added to the language.

Did you notice I said *fresh crop?* More about that in a moment.

A cliché is an overworked, overtired expression. For instance, I don't want to hear another politician in my lifetime say, "At the end of the day." But I know I will, so when the dust settles I'll move on to greener pastures. (Clichés in the last sentence are there for satirical purposes only).

The best time to look for clichés is when you are revising. You can cut them, say the same thing in another way, or on occasion freshen them up. Like the Harlan Ellison line referenced earlier: *She looked like a million bucks tax free.*

Now, getting back to *fresh crop.* Sometimes a familiar phrase can operate as a shorthand. It makes the point and gets out of the way. People understand it. It's not offensive to the ear. So don't beat yourself up (there's another!) if some of them are sprinkled in your text.

But do ask yourself if it's the best way to make the point.

You make the call.

(The above line is a familiar phrase, but it fits, so it stays!)

Creative Copying

In a 2012 keynote address at The University of the Arts, Neil Gaiman spoke about creativity. At one point he said, "The urge, starting out, is to copy. And that's not a bad thing. Most of us only find our own voices after we've sounded like a lot of other people."

That's a solid bit of wisdom. Many great writers of the past spent time copying other authors' works. Not plagiarizing, but writing down the words to learn sentence structure and rhythm.

In the next part of this book I provide examples of voice in different genres. When you read a passage you admire, pause and read it out loud. If you really like it, copy it. Type it out or, even better, use pen and paper. You stretch your range that way. All of this can then be filtered through you as you create voice on your own pages.

The full quote from Gaiman in that keynote is as follows:

> The urge, starting out, is to copy. And that's not a bad thing. Most of us only find our own voices after we've sounded like a lot of other people. But the one thing that you have that nobody else has is you. Your voice, your mind, your story, your vision. So write and draw and build and play and dance and live as only you can.

Now have a look at voice in different genres.

Literary Examples

What exactly is literary fiction?

Some people describe it in the negative: it is not commercial fiction. In other words, it does not follow genre conventions.

Others say that literary fiction is more concerned with *style* than other forms.

Still others hold that lit-fic is more about the inner life of a character than the outer form of the plot.

Regardless, as with any other type of fiction, voice is the secret ingredient, the X factor that elevates the story.

Example 1: From *On the Road* by Jack Kerouac:

> It was remarkable how Dean could go mad and then suddenly continue with his soul—which I think is wrapped up in a fast car, a coast to reach, and a woman at the end of the road—calmly and sanely as though nothing had happened. "I get like that every time in Denver now—I can't make that town any more. Gookly, goody, Dean's a spooky. Zoom!" I told him I had been over this Nebraska road before in '47. He had too. "Sal, when I was working for the New Era Laundry in Los Angeles, nineteen forty-four, falsifying my age, I made a trip to Indianapolis Speedway for the express purpose of seeing the Memorial Day classic hitch, hiking by day and stealing cars by night to make time. Also I had a twenty-dollar Buick back in LA, my first car, it couldn't pass the brake and light inspection so I decided I needed an out-of-state license to pirate the car without arrest so went through here to get the license. As I was hitchhiking through one of these very towns, with

the plates concealed under my coat, a nosy sheriff who thought I was pretty young to be hitchhiking accosted me on the main drag. He found the plates and threw me in the two-cell jail with a county delinquent who should have been in the home for the old since he couldn't feed himself (the sheriff's wife fed him) and sat through the day drooling and slobbering. After investigation, which included corny things like a fatherly quiz, then an abrupt turnabout to frighten me with threats, a comparison of my handwriting, et cetera, and after I made the most magnificent speech of my life to get out of it, concluding with the confession that I was lying about my car-stealing past and was only looking for my paw who was a farmhand hereabouts, he let me go. Of course I missed the races. The following fall I did the same thing again to see the Notre Dame-California game in South Bend, Indiana—trouble none of this time and, Sal, I had just the money for the ticket and not an extra cent and didn't eat anything all up and back except for what I could panhandle from all kinds of crazy cats I met on the road and at the same time gun gals. Only guy in the United States of America that ever went to so much trouble to see a ballgame."

Comment

That's the energy of the book. But notice where the voice comes from. It's capturing the wild mind of Dean Moriarty (the fictional name of a real friend of Kerouac's, Neal Cassady). Kerouac's novel is autobiographical. He wanted to convey what being on the road felt like to him (Sal Paradise in the book), especially when in the thrall of the larger-than-life Cassady.

It is legend that Kerouac produced much of *On the Road* in fits of manic typing, setting it down on a roll of butcher paper so he wouldn't have to pause to change sheets. In this case it was a matter of trying to write in the same frame of mind as the Beats tried to live. He was once asked to describe his style of writing. He called it "Be-bop prose rhapsody."

Here is the most famous passage from *On the Road:*

The only people for me are the mad ones, the ones who are mad to live, mad to talk, mad to be saved, desirous of everything at the same time, the ones who never yawn or say a commonplace thing, but burn, burn, burn, like fabulous yellow roman candles exploding like spiders across the stars and in the middle you see the blue centerlight pop and everybody goes "Awww!"

Kerouac once jotted down his "beliefs" about writing. I reproduce them here because I've used them myself as writing prompts for getting at voice and style. They are as follows, with Kerouac's own spelling preserved:

1. Scribbled secret notebooks, and wild typewritten pages, for yr own joy
2. Submissive to everything, open, listening
3. Try never get drunk outside yr own house
4. Be in love with yr life
5. Something that you feel will find its own form
6. Be crazy dumbsaint of the mind
7. Blow as deep as you want to blow
8. Write what you want bottomless from bottom of the mind
9. The unspeakable visions of the individual
10. No time for poetry but exactly what is
11. Visionary tics shivering in the chest
12. In tranced fixation dreaming upon object before you
13. Remove literary, grammatical and syntactical inhibition
14. Like Proust be an old teahead of time
15. Telling the true story of the world in interior monolog
16. The jewel center of interest is the eye within the eye
17. Write in recollection and amazement for yourself
18. Work from pithy middle eye out, swimming in language sea
19. Accept loss forever
20. Believe in the holy contour of life
21. Struggle to sketch the flow that already exists intact in mind

22. Dont think of words when you stop but to see picture better

23. Keep track of every day the date emblazoned in yr morning

24. No fear or shame in the dignity of yr experience, language & knowledge

25. Write for the world to read and see yr exact pictures of it

26. Bookmovie is the movie in words, the visual American form

27. In praise of Character in the Bleak inhuman Loneliness

28. Composing wild, undisciplined, pure, coming in from under, crazier the better

29. You're a Genius all the time

29. Writer-Director of Earthly movies Sponsored & Angeled in Heaven

Example 2: From Pulitzer Prize winning author Stephen Millhouser's story, "Miracle Polish":

> I should have said no to the stranger at the door, with his skinny throat and his black sample case that pulled him a little to the side, so that one of his jacket cuffs was higher than the other, a polite no would have done the trick, no thanks, I'm afraid not, not today, then the closing of the door and the heavy click of the latch, but I'd seen the lines of dirt in the black shoe-creases, the worn-down heels, the shine on the jacket sleeves, the glint of desperation in his eyes.

Comment

This is the opening paragraph, and it is one, long sentence. It starts off with an ominous phrase, *I should have said no to the stranger at the door...* which makes us want to read on. Then the cascading words after that establish a momentum, a feeling like the moments before a car crash where you can't stop the motion and know it's going to end badly.

Then it is Millhouser's selection of detail that grabs us. Each one establishing just a little bit of discomfort. Not, I should add, anything that is immediately off-putting or horrific. Millhouser isn't after that. He wants to slowly pull us in with increasing notes of unease.

skinny throat
pulled him a little to one side
one of his jacket cuffs was higher than the other
lines of dirt in the black shoe-creases
worn-down heels
shine on the jacket sleeves
glint of desperation

Great literary fiction lives by such telling details, and the sound of the words.

Mystery and Noir Examples

The hard-boiled school of writing is also sometimes labeled crime or noir fiction. Or, if the lead character is an investigator of some kind, detective fiction or PI (private investigator) fiction.

This is the land of the urban underbelly, the criminals and their pursuers. It rocketed to popularity after the publication of Dashiell Hammett's masterpiece, *The Maltese Falcon* (1929). This was also the beginning of the golden age of pulp magazines, such as *Black Mask* and *Dime Detective*. Every month a voracious reading public gobbled up stories of tough guys, dames, gats, cops, gumshoes, and capers.

After World War II, this style of writing found a natural home in the exploding paperback market. Writers such as Jim Thompson, Ross Macdonald, John D. MacDonald, William Campbell Gault, David Goodis, and scores of others were able to make a living churning out hard boiled novels.

Below are a few examples:

Example 1: From *The Postman Always Rings Twice* by James M. Cain:

> They threw me off the hay truck about noon. I had swung on the night before, down at the border, and as soon as I got up there under the canvas, I went to sleep. I needed plenty of that, after three weeks in Tia Juana, and I was still getting it when they pulled off to one side to let the engine cool. They saw a foot sticking out and threw me off. I tried some comical stuff, but all I got was a dead pan, so that gag

was out. They gave me a cigarette, though, and I hiked down the road to find something to eat.

Comment

Cain's 1934 novella (at about 35,000 words) became a huge hit and influence on writers of the hard boiled school. Notice how fast it starts. A guy gets thrown off a truck after sneaking a ride. He hasn't got money. He bums a cigarette and then goes off to find something to eat.

He's what they used to call a bum. Trouble follows such men in noir, and a couple of pages later:

> Then I saw her. She had been out back, in the kitchen, but she came in to gather up my dishes. Except for the shape, she really wasn't any raving beauty, but she had a sulky look to her, and her lips stuck out in a way that made me want to mash them in for her.

The sentences are short, action-packed. They come at you like the slugs from a .38.

When Raymond Chandler came along, he elevated the voice of noir by adding his own stamp to it, in a big way. Take a look.

Example 2: From the short story "Red Wind" by Raymond Chandler

> There was a desert wind blowing that night. It was one of those hot dry Santa Anas that come down through the mountain passes and curl your hair and make your nerves jump and your skin itch. On nights like that every booze party ends in a fight. Meek little wives feel the edge of the carving knife and study their husbands' necks. Anything can happen.

Comment

Stylistically, this is clearly Chandler's voice. It's Omniscient narration, setting a mood for the story to come.

This is a legitimate fiction move, by the way. You can start a novel or story with a sort of "wide angle establishing shot." Then pull in closer to the POV character.

I can't resist giving you, however, my favorite Chandler line. It's from *Farewell, My Lovely* in the First Person voice of Chandler's detective hero, Philip Marlowe:

> It was a blonde. A blonde to make a bishop kick a hole in a stained glass window.

In that same vein, one more Chandler excerpt. If you have a First Person narrator, don't hesitate to use that voice to establish tone and scene. Some of the most memorable passages in hard-boiled fiction are like this one from *The High Window*:

> Bunker Hill is old town, lost town, shabby town, crook town. Once, very long ago, it was the choice residential district of the city, and there are still standing a few of the jigsaw Gothic mansions with wide porches and walls covered with round-end shingles and full corner bay windows with spindle turrets. They are all rooming houses now, their parquetry floors are scratched and worn through the once glossy finish, and the wide sweeping staircases are dark with time and cheap varnish laid on over generations of dirt. In the tall rooms haggard landladies bicker with shifty tenants. On the wide cool front porches, reaching their cracked shoes into the sun, and staring at nothing, sit the old men with faces like lost battles.
>
> In and around the old houses there are flyblown restaurants and Italian fruit stands and cheap apartment houses and little candy stores where you can buy even nastier things than their candy. And there are ratty hotels where nobody except people named Smith and Jones sign the register and where the night clerk is half watchdog and half pander.

Out of the apartment houses come women who should be young but have faces like stale beer; men with pulled-down hats and quick eyes that look the street over behind the cupped hand that shields the match flame; worn intellectuals with cigarette coughs and no money in the bank; fly cops with granite faces and unwavering eyes; cokies and coke peddlers; people who look like nothing in particular and know it, and once in a while even men that actually go to work. But they come out early, when the wide cracked sidewalks are empty and still have dew on them.

Example 3: From *Don't Cry For Me* by William Campbell Gault:

I was sick. Not from liquor or cigarettes or hamburger or Ellen or beer. I was just sick of Pete Worden, who couldn't grow up, who couldn't go out and peddle insurance or real estate or golf clubs and settle down in Westchester or some equally inane section and become another semi-contented nonentity.

The rest of the boys were doing it; who the hell did I think I was? It was time to grow up and be nothing. On the hundred I got from the estate, and with what a job would bring, I'd get by nicely in the middle-class suburbs.

As a matter of fact, if I did get a job and settle down, I'd get my share of the estate from John. And my share was half. I had no idea what that would be, but his half kept John in the upper strata, and my half should do as much for me.

And with Ellen I could even take Westchester. There wasn't any sense in kidding myself; the bed and the dice and the bottle were my symbols and the greatest of these was the bed.

They'd made a vulgarity out of the bed with their false shame and their fear-born standards, but name me a higher ecstasy or a truer communion. Shallow, Pete Worden, superficial, unlearned, vulgar, and aggressive.

And in love.

In love, but would I be? Day after day the same girl? In curlers and cold cream, pregnant or with the sniffles, at the country-club dance or the P.T.A. meeting, making the small daily surrenders, making the big and little adjustments that went into the long haul? With my foul temper, with my insatiable need for affection, could I plod it out without killing it?

I doubted it like hell. Even with Ellen.

Comment

What is most apparent here is *emotion*. When you write in First Person, you need attitude and emotion. The reader relates to the character with hot blood coursing through his veins.

So try this: Select a passage of your novel where your narrator is expressing emotion (or, if in Third Person, where the emotion is strong).

Then kick everything up twenty-five percent. Put more into it, more emotion, more passion.

Thriller Examples

What is the difference between a mystery and a thriller? I like to put it this way: a mystery is about trying to find out who did it. It's like a maze. The protagonist goes from clue to clue trying to piece things together.

The thriller feels more like *Will it happen again? And soon? To the hero?* And if he doesn't stop whoever is doing the bad stuff, more people—maybe a whole universe!—will be harmed.

Instead of a maze, a thriller feels like you're forced to run over a mine field.

Character is important in any novel, and that includes thrillers. But once we are bonded, we want to be worried about the compactor. Action scenes take on special importance.

Example 1: *The Hunger Games* by Suzanne Collins

A few hours later, the stampede of feet shakes me from slumber. I look around in bewilderment. It's not yet dawn, but my stinging eyes can see it.

It would be hard to miss the wall of fire descending on me.

My first impulse is to scramble from the tree, but I'm belted in. Somehow my fumbling fingers release the buckle and I fall to the ground in a heap, still snarled in my sleeping bag. There's no time for any kind of packing. Fortunately, my backpack and water bottle are already in the bag. I shove in the belt, hoist the bag over my shoulder, and flee.

The world has transformed to flame and smoke. Burning branches crack from trees and fall in showers of sparks at my feet. All I can do is follow the others, the rabbits and deer, and I even spot a wild dog pack shooting through the woods. I trust their sense of direction because their instincts are sharper than mine. But they are much faster, flying through the underbrush so gracefully as my boots catch on roots and fallen tree limbs, that there's no way I can keep apace with them.

The heat is horrible, but worse than the heat is the smoke, which threatens to suffocate me at any moment. I pull the top of my shirt up over my nose, grateful to find it soaked in sweat, and it offers a thin veil of protection. And I run, choking, my bag banging against my back, my face cut with branches that materialize from the gray haze without warning, because I know I am supposed to run.

Comment

Notice the attention to detail in the midst of the action. The more vivid you can make the reality, the better. With good, solid tension like this, stretch things out to the max. This scene goes on for another couple of pages. Keep the readers flipping––or *swiping*––pages!

Example 2: *The Good Guy* by Dean Koontz

He needed to look at her and he dreaded looking at her, and he didn't know why or how, within minutes of their meeting, she should have become the focus of either need or dread. He had never felt like this before, and although a thousand songs and movies had programmed him to call it love, he knew it wasn't love. He wasn't a man who fell in love at first sight. Besides, love didn't have such an element of mortal terror as was a part of this feeling.

Comment

I used this clip as a reminder that character feelings are a vital part of making us care. Koontz is a master at this. He pauses to show us his lead experiencing a feeling like love, but it is bound by words like *dread* and *mortal terror.* The mood stays tense. Good cross-currents of emotion in the midst of the action.

Fantasy Examples

Voice in fantasy fiction has to evoke a certain sense of wonder. It may be "dark" wonder or "light" wonder, but because it's a place of magic, there must be an otherworldly sense created for the reader.

The key is to weave the wonder. Make it part of the fabric of the narrative. As these examples show:

Example 1: *The Lion, The Witch, and the Wardrobe* by C. S. Lewis:

> When [Aslan] said, "We have a long journey to go. You must ride on me." And he crouched down and the children climbed onto his warm, golden back, and Susan sat first, holding on tightly to his mane and Lucy sat behind holding on tightly to Susan. And with a great heave he rose underneath them and then shot off, faster than any horse could go, down hill and into the thick of the forest.
>
> That ride was perhaps the most wonderful thing that happened to them in Narnia. Have you ever had a gallop on a horse? Think of that; and then take away the heavy noise of the hoofs and the jingle of the bits and imagine instead the almost noiseless padding of the great paws. Then imagine instead of the black or grey or chestnut back of the horse the soft roughness of golden fur, and the mane flying back in the wind. And then imagine you are going about twice as fast as the fastest racehorse. But this is a mount that doesn't need to be guided and never grows tired. He rushes on and on, never missing his footing, never hesitating, threading his way with perfect skill between tree trunks, jumping over bush and briar and the smaller

streams, wading the larger, swimming the largest of all. And you are riding not on a road nor in a park nor even on the downs, but right across Narnia, in spring, down solemn avenues of beech and across sunny glades of oak, through wild orchards of snow-white cherry trees, past roaring waterfalls and mossy rocks and echoing caverns, up windy slopes alight with gorse bushes, and across the shoulders of heathery mountains and along giddy ridges and down, down, down again into wild valleys and out into acres of blue flowers.

Comment

One added wrinkle here is that Lewis was writing primarily for children. Thus, the narrative is written to captivate a child's imagination, to the point where Lewis as the author directly addresses the reader. Note the specificity of detail. This is crucial in a fantasy because you must build a world, and the world will not be convincing without detail.

Example 2: *The Name of the Wind* by Patrick Rothfuss

It was one of those perfect autumn days so common in stories and so rare in the real world. The weather was warm and dry, ideal for ripening a field of wheat or corn. On both sides of the road the trees were changing color. Tall poplars had gone a buttery yellow while the shrubby sumac encroaching on the road was tinged with a violent red. Only the old oaks seemed reluctant to give up the summer and their leaves remained and even mingling of gold and green.

Everything said, you couldn't hope for a nicer day to have half a dozen ex-soldiers with hunting bows relieve you of everything you owned.

Comment

Like Lewis, Rothfuss also addresses the reader, only in the

more adult style of Omniscient narrator. But note how he grounds the world in specific detail. Even though there is no fantasy element in the paragraph, that world has already been established in the book. What the realistic details do is take the magic and make it as real as everyday life.

Example 3: *On a Pale Horse* by Piers Anthony

> The proprietor affected shock. "Sir, I would not handle black magic! All my spells are genuine white magic."
>
> "Black magic knows no law except its own," Zane muttered.
>
> "White magic!" the proprietor insisted. "My wares are certified genuine white."
>
> But such certificates, Zane knew, were only as good as the person who made them. White magic was always honest, for it stemmed from God, but black magic often masqueraded as white. Naturally Satan, the Father of Lies, sought to deceive people about his wares. It was hard for an amateur to distinguish reliably between magics. Of course, he could have this stone separately appraised, and the appraisal would include a determination of its magical status—but that would be expensive, and he would have to buy it first. If the verdict turned out negative, he would still be stuck.
>
> The star hovered over Zane's shoe. "Lift your foot, sir," the proprietor suggested. Zane raised his foot, and the star slipped under like a scurrying insect.

Comment

The above was text was written as if it could have taken place as a conversation in a common drug store. That's a great touch, when you can make a fantasy world seem as real as the world we live in now.

Science Fiction Examples

As with fantasy, science fiction revolves around making an "other world" understandable and relatable. Because it relies heavily on things scientific and technical, there can be a temptation to drop in a lot of esoteric information all at once––what writers call a "dump."

Instead, integration of the research in a natural fashion is a big key to the SF voice.

Example 1: *Nemesis* by Isaac Asimov

Marlene had last seen the Solar System when she was a little over one year old. She didn't remember it, of course.

She had read a great deal about it, but none of the reading had ever made her feel that it could ever have been part of her, nor she a part of it.

In all her fifteen years of life, she remembered only Rotor. She had always thought of it as a large world. It was eight kilometers across, after all. Every once in a while since she was ten—once a month when she could manage it— she had walked around it for the exercise, and sometimes had taken the low-gravity paths so she could skim a little. that was always fun. Skim or walk, Rotor went on and on, with its buildings, its parks, its farms, and mostly its people.

It took her a whole day to do it, but her mother didn't mind. She said Rotor was perfectly safe. "Not like Earth," she would say but she wouldn't say *why* Earth was not safe. "Never mind," she would say.

It was the people Marlene liked least. The new census, they said, would show sixty thousand of them on Rotor.

Too many. Far too many. Every one of them showing a false face. Marlene hated seeing those false faces and knowing there was something different inside. Nor could she say anything about it. She had tried sometimes when she had been younger, but her mother had grown angry and told her she must never say things like that.

Comment

Isaac Asimov developed a very utilitarian style, on purpose. He wanted to get out of the way of the story and also be able to write quickly. Yet he also manages to do what the best SF does: weave the elements seamlessly into the narrative, while also capturing the feel of the character, a young girl.

Example 2: *Saturn Run* by John Sandford and Ctein

February 9, 2066

From ten kilometers out, the Sky Survey Observatory looked like an oversized beer can. Yellow-white sunlight glittered from the can's outward side, while the other half was a shifting funhouse reflection of the pale blues and pearly cloud streaks of the earth, a thousand kilometers below.

The can was not quite alone: an egg-shaped service module, human-sized, encrusted with insectile appendages, ports, windows, and cameras, was closing in on it. Storage lockers and canisters surrounded the base of the egg. Had there been any air around it, and anything with ears, the faint twang of country music might have been heard vibrating through its ice-white walls: "Oh, my ATV is a hustlin' on down the line, and them tofu critters are looking mighty fine . . ."

The handyman was making a house call.

The Sky Survey Observatory carried four telescopes: the Big Eye, the Medium Eye, the Small Eye, and Chuck's

Eye, the latter unofficially named after a congressman who slipped the funding into a veto-proof Social Security bill. The scopes stared outward, assisted by particle and radiation detectors, looking for interesting stuff.

All of the SSO's remotely operable telescopes, radio dishes, and particle sensors, all the digital cameras and computers, all the storage systems and fuel tanks and solar cells, lived at the command of astronomers sitting comfortably in climate-controlled offices back on the ground.

Until the observatory broke. Then somebody had to go there with the metaphorical equivalent of a screwdriver.

One of the groundhuggers called, "Can you see it?"

Comment

What I like about this passage is the way it mixes the mundane with the futuristic. A sky observatory that looks like a beer can. A country song. Nicknames for the telescopes, the way we'd do it if we were handymen in space. And all of the description leads naturally into the action, which begins with the first line of dialogue.

Horror Examples

With horror, the voice is one of impending doom, dark shadows, goose bumps, outright terror, and (in the case of writers like Stephen King) the occasional gross-out. The writing does not have to be graphic; indeed, some of the best horror writing is merely suggestive, as in the ghost stories of M. R. James.

Example 1: *The Shining* by Stephen King

> His breath stopped in a gasp. An almost drowsy terror stole through his veins. Yes. Yes. There was something in here with him, some awful thing the Overlook had saved for just such a chance as this. Maybe a huge spider that had burrowed down under the dead leaves, or a rat ... or maybe the corpse of some little kid that had died here on the playground. Had that ever happened?
>
> At the far end of the concrete ring, Danny heard the stealthy crackle of dead leaves, as something came for him on its hands and knees.

Comment

Notice that it is the *unseen* thing that brings the dread. It's the same principle Steven Spielberg used in *Jaws*. The first hour or so of the film you never see the shark, just what the shark does and how people react.

And the sense of dread is filtered through Danny, so the narrative takes on his inner voice. It's all directed at how this situation would feel *to him*.

Example 2: The ghost story "Slaughter House" by Richard Matheson

> But then began the little things, the intangible things, the things without reason.
>
> Walking on the stairs, in the hallway, through the rooms, Saul or I, singly or together, would stop and receive the strangest impulse in our minds; of fleeting moment yet quite definite while existent.
>
> It is difficult to express the feeling with adequate clarity. It was as if we heard something although there was no sound, as though we saw something when there was nothing before the eye. A sense of shifting presence, delicate and tenuous, hidden from all physical senses and yet, somehow, perceived.
>
> There was no explaining it. In point of fact we never spoke of it together. It was too nebulous a feeling to discuss, incapable of being materialized into words. Restless though it made us, there was no mutual comparison of sensation nor could there be. Even the most abstract of thought formation could not approach what we were experiencing.
>
> Sometimes I would come upon Saul casting a hurried glance over his shoulder, or surreptitiously reaching out to stroke empty air as though he expected his fingers to touch some invisible entity. Sometimes he would catch me doing the same. On occasion we would smile awkwardly, both of us appreciating the moment without words.

Comment

Matheson creates a rather stuffy sounding narrator, so the voice expresses the same dread of the unseen as Danny in *The Shining,* but different in tone. It's also a period piece, which requires a distinct and old-fashioned type of speech. Matheson carries it off without a hitch. The CAP Method is on marvelous display in this story.

Romance Examples

R omance writing, as you know, emphasizes feelings. The reader has to be drawn into the love story, has to *want* the lovers to get together. That's the main task of the romance writer then—to get us bonded to the characters so we will want to follow them on their journey to *amour*.

Example 1: *Secret Star* by Nora Roberts

> She watched him tuck his badge back into his pocket, while those unreadable cop's eyes skimmed over her face. Memorizing features, she thought, irritated. Making mental notes of any distinguishing marks. Just what the hell was going on?
>
> "Yes, I'm Grace Fontaine. This is my property, my home. And as you're in it, without a proper warrant, you're trespassing. As calling a cop seems superfluous, maybe I'll just call my lawyer."
>
> He angled his head, and unwilling caught a whiff of that siren's scent of hers. Perhaps it was that, and feeling its instant and unwelcome effect on his system, that had him speaking without thought.
>
> "Well, Ms. Fontaine, you look damn good for a dead woman."

Comment

This is a common romance trope, the initial meeting of the lovers that throws negative sparks. Roberts does this as well as anybody. But did you notice that she switched POV right in the middle? We start off in Grace's head, but then we move into the head of the man (Seth) because we are told what he smells and how he feels about it.

This method is called "head hopping" and was once fairly common, especially in romance writing. These days, however, editors and readers seem to prefer the rule of one POV per scene.

Example 2: *The Inn at Rose Harbor* by Debbie Macomber

Contrary to what I'd been told about visitation dreams, Paul did nothing to reassure me he was at peace. Instead, he stood before me in full military gear. He was surrounded by a light that was so bright it was hard to look at him. Even so, I found it impossible to turn away.

I wanted to run to him but was afraid that if I moved, he would disappear. I couldn't bear to lose him again even if this was only an apparition.

At first he didn't speak. I didn't either, unsure of what I could or should say. I remember that emotion filled my eyes with tears and I covered my mouth for fear I would cry out.

He joined me then and took me in his arms, holding me close and running his hand down the back of my head, comforting me. I clung to him, unwilling to let him go. Over and over he whispered gentle words of love.

When the lump in my throat eased, I looked up at him and our eyes met. It felt as though he was alive and we needed to catch up after a long absence. There was so much I wanted to tell him, so much I wanted him to explain. The fact that he'd had such a large life insurance policy had come as a shock. At first I'd felt guilty about accepting such a large amount of cash. Shouldn't that money go to his family? But his mother was dead, and his father had remarried and lived in Australia. They had never been especially close. The lawyer told me Paul had been clear in his instructions.

In my dream I wanted to tell Paul that I'd used the

money to buy this bed-and-breakfast and that I'd named it after him. One of the first improvements I wanted to make was to plant a rose garden with a bench and an arbor. But in the dream, I said none of that because it seemed like he already knew.

He brushed the hair from my forehead and kissed me there ever so gently.

"You've chosen well," he whispered, his eyes warm with love. "In time you'll know joy again."

Comment

Macomber is a master at evoking emotion, not too much, and not too little. Here, she combines backstory material with a vivid dream about a dead husband, weaving exposition and emotion seamlessly in the passage. When done well, especially in the romance genre, it is most effective.

YA Examples

Young Adult fiction continues to be a hot slice of the publishing pie. It's a wide-ranging genre, where the protagonists are teens and deal with any contemporary youth issue there is—friendships, envy, sex, self-worth, parental divorce, school, bullies, depression, catastrophic illness, and on and on.

A great number of YA books are written in First Person POV. And a number of those are written in *present tense* First Person, as in the following.

Example 1: *The Sky is Everywhere* by Jandy Nelson

I have seen him, because when I return to my band seat, the one I've occupied for the last year, he's in it. Even in the stun of grief, my eyes roam from the black boots, up the miles of legs covered in denim, over the endless torso, and finally settle on a face so animated I wonder if I've interrupted a conversation between him and my music stand.

"Hi," he says, and jumps up. He's treetop tall. "You must be Lennon." He points to my name on the chair. "I heard about—I'm sorry." I notice the way he holds his clarinet, not precious with it, tight fist around the neck, like a sword.

"Thank you," I say, and every available inch of his face busts into a smile--whoa. Has he blown into our school on a gust of wind from another world? The guy looks unabashedly jack-o'-lantern happy, which couldn't be more foreign to the sullen demeanor most of us strove to perfect.

Comment

First Person, present tense, renders the action immediate. But notice, too, the attitude in the voice. Attitude in First Person is the most important thing. You'll find all sorts of opinions on the merits, or lack thereof, of First Person present. It seems most acceptable these days in YA, but it's not the only choice. Let's take a look at a YA that is in First Person past tense.

Example 2: *The Beginning of Everything* by Robyn Schneider

I don't know why people say "hit by a car," as though the other vehicle physically lashes out like some sort of champion boxer. What hit me first was my airbag, and then my steering wheel, and I suppose the driver's side door and whatever that part is called that your knee jams up against.

The impact was deafening, and everything just seemed to slam toward me and crunch. There was the stink of my engine dying under the front hood, like burnt rubber, but salty and metallic. Everyone rushed out onto the Beideckers' lawn, which was two houses down, and through the engine smoke, I could see an army of girls in strapless dresses, their phones raised, solemnly snapping pictures of the wreck.

But I just sat there laughing and unscathed because I'm an immortal, hundred-year-old vampire.

All right, I'm screwing with you. Because it would have been awesome if I'd been able to shake it off and drive away, like that ass weasel who never even stopped after laying into my Z4.

Comment

This is First Person, past tense, and the author loses nothing. Notice also how the narrator addresses readers directly, adding a personal and one-on-one dimension to the storytelling. It's what the theatre world calls "breaking the fourth wall," meaning an actor looks at the audience and speaks or reacts to it. The YA audience responds well to this kind of intimacy.

For Further Reading

Voice truly is the secret power in great writing.
Pedestrian prose is serviceable, but ultimately forgettable. There's plenty of plain, ordinary writing out there in the vast sea of content.

But when you can stand out with something *more*, readers will be pleased by the effect.

Voice is the more.

If this book has been helpful to you, please take a moment to leave a review.

And for your further study, here are a few books relevant to our topic that I've found helpful:

Description by Monica Wood (Writer's Digest Books)
Word Painting by Rebecca McClanahan (Writer's Digest Books)
Making Shapely Fiction by Jerome Stern (W. W. Norton)
Zen in the Art of Writing by Ray Bradbury (Capra Press)

I'd also love to have you sign up for my email updates. You'll be the first to know about my book releases and special deals. My emails are short and I won't stuff your mailbox, and you can certainly unsubscribe at any time. If you do sign up, I'll put your name in the random drawing I do each month for a free book of mine.

Sign up by going to my website: www.jamesscottbell.com. And keep writing!

More of my writing books:

Plot & Structure

Write Your Novel From the Middle
Plot & Structure
Super Structure
Conflict & Suspense

Revision

Revision & Self-Editing

Dialogue

How to Write Dazzling Dialogue

Publishing & Career

How to Make a Living as a Writer
The Art of War for Writers
Self-Publishing Attack!

Writing & The Writing Life

Writing Fiction for All You're Worth
Fiction Attack!

My Website

JamesScottBell.com

28519544R00068

Made in the USA
Middletown, DE
18 January 2016